D0984525

Jude P. Dougherty

THE LOGIC OF
RELIGION

* * *

The Catholic University of America Press
Washington, D.C.

The paper used in this publication meets the minimum
requirements of American National Standards for
Information Science—Permanence of Paper for Printed
Library materials, ANSI Z39.48-1984.
∞

LIBRARY OF CONGRESS CATALOGING-IN-PUBLICATION DATA
Dougherty, Jude P., 1930–
    The logic of religion / by Jude P. Dougherty.
        p. cm.
    Includes bibliographical references and index.
    ISBN 0-8132-1308-8 (pbk. : alk. paper)
    1. Religion—Philosophy.   I. Title.
BL51 .D62 2003
200—dc21
                                                         2002020113

Contents

RELIGION AS AN OBJECT OF
PHILOSOPHICAL STUDY

The focus of this study is Western religion. The word "religion" is itself a Latin word, and its meaning is to be found in the classical texts where it is first employed. The concept itself antedates the word. We find extended discussions of religion in antiquity and later in the Middle Ages. In the chapters which follow, many authors could have been canvassed for their views, but it serves the purpose of this inquiry to consider the thought of a representative few, beginning in antiquity with Socrates, Plato, Cicero, and Seneca and then moving to the Middle Ages as represented by Augustine, Averroes, and Aquinas. By examining their analysis of religion, we gain insight into the nature and logic of religion before and after the advent of Christianity. Subsequent investigation will lead us to consider the work of David Hume, Immanuel Kant, and G. W. F. Hegel. In their philosophies we find not only an account of the logic of religion but an appreciation of its implications in the social order.

This historical excursion is valuable because the history of philosophy is much more a part of philosophy than the history of science is a part of science. No one can proceed very far on his own philosophical reflection unless he first studies the history of the discipline. That history first appears as a chronicle of mutually destructive systems, but beneath the conflict one can find a thread of intelligibility. Western philosophy itself is a chronicle of Western man's grappling with the transcendent, both affirming and denying the reality of an immaterial order. The philosophers selected for consideration here have been chosen for their dogmatic significance, each representing an attempt to deal with the realm of being and subsequently of religion from a distinctive philosophical vantage point or methodology.

Questions of methodology and definition could easily absorb the whole of this brief volume. That said, a few remarks are nevertheless in order. This volume is not meant to provide a history of Western religion or to examine in detail the thought of any of the philosophers considered for discussion. Its purpose will be served by a cursory review of Greek and Roman attitudes toward the divine, followed by an examination of the distinctive features of Christianity and the use of Greek philosophy by the Fathers of the Church as they attempted to understand the message of the Gospel and the Hebrew Scriptures. Examined also is the split within Christianity occasioned by the Protestant Reformation, and finally the Enlightenment repudiation of Christianity itself. This study may be regarded as a survey of how believers and nonbelievers view the social phenomenon we call religion. Attention is briefly paid to selected Oriental modes of thought, some properly called religion in the Western sense, some more akin to philosophical rather than religious outlooks.

From a contemporary perspective the word "religion" may be difficult to define in such a way that it is applicable to all the phenomena which are popularly called religious. No one is likely to deny that Christianity, Judaism, and Mohammedanism are religions. Shinto is likewise a religion in the Western sense, but Buddhism and Brahmanism are not religions in the same sense although they are often called religions. Buddha's doctrine clearly advances an asceticism, but it is atheistic at its core, just as Brahmanism is pantheistic. Similarly, the trappings associated with religion are not to be confused with religion itself. Socially conducted ritual, symbolic and formal, need not be religious. The Japanese worship of the emperor, for example, is a patriotic not a religious act. The cult of reason fostered by Robespierre in the aftermath of the French Revolution was decidedly antireligious although its rituals mimicked Christianity. Thus, rites, vestments, temples, and moral teaching can be nonreligious as well as religious in character.

The title of this book, following the lead of Joseph Bochenski's brief work of the same title,[1] has been chosen to distinguish it from many other philosophical works focused on religion. Readers will recognize that the term "philosophy of religion" is commonly employed as a title for books and college courses, but there is no agreement among authors with respect to the nature of the discipline. The concept of the discipline employed here, while not unique, is not shared by all who write under that title. A few preliminary distinctions are in order. First, the philosophy of religion is to be distinguished from the psychology of religion and the history of religion, even though the philosophy of religion necessarily draws upon the data or testimony supplied by those disciplines. In the view entertained here, religion is examined just like any other social institution. Its rational structure is to be examined, its origins explored, its doctrines established, its social value appraised. Philosophy does not pronounce on the truth of religion but rather observes, describes, and analyzes religious manifestations as objects in themselves. In examining the observed facts of religion as

1. J. M. Bochenski, The Logic of Religion (New York: New York University Press, 1965).

expressed in language and gesture, it suspends judgment regarding whether they actually refer to a transcendent reality. The act of religious faith comes within the scope of philosophical analysis only insofar as philosophy can examine the causes or grounds of the act of belief. But this type of inquiry is not to be confused with natural theology, sometimes called the "philosophy of God" or "theodicy." Some questions which traditionally were raised in natural theology (i.e., whether God exists, whether anything can be known of His nature) have in recent decades been addressed as if they were part of the philosophy of religion. To scan the contents of many books called the "philosophy of religion" is to find examinations of St. Anselm's ontological argument, St. Thomas's five ways, discussions of analogy, and examinations of "religious experience." Those discussions do not find a place in this volume.

Some philosophers, particularly those schooled in the British analytic tradition, begin their study of religion by focusing on "religious speech" or "religious language." This study does not because there is something more fundamental. True, the religious person uses speech in worship and in expressing himself with respect to the object of worship, but it is his intention, his insights which are to be examined. One may examine religious speech as one may examine the poetry of a given period in English history. It may be beautiful and effective, or it may not. The language employed by religious persons examined as poetry is a literary study, and while certain philosophical principles may be employed in its pursuit, it is not philosophy proper. Religion, it is acknowledged, can test one's theory of language. Whether God exists or not, given a conception of God as transcendent, one can ask how that transcendence can be captured in language, and the ensuing puzzle can challenge even the best minds.

There is obviously no one philosophical perspective from which to consider the nature of religion. Agreement on the nature of the discipline is no more to be expected than agreement about the parameters of the philosophy of science. Yet a philosophical perspective on religion should at least be definable, and a truly philosophical vantage point should prescind from subscription to a religious viewpoint. One may have difficulties in taking a detached view. One either is a believer or he is not. Similarly, one does not have to regard religion and its claims as something intrinsically absurd. Obviously, one's general philosophical outlook colors one's attitude toward religion. As one begins to analyze religion from a philosophical viewpoint, there are three basic positions one can take: that of the atheist, that of the agnostic, or that of the believer—although these positions are hardly ever pure. Thoroughgoing atheists are rare. There are few who philosophically argue that God does not exist. Most philosophers, if they do not affirm that God is, maintain simply that there is no evidence that he does exist. The believer, on the other hand, will affirm that God is—quite apart from evidence—though some believers may argue that this faith is well grounded because it is corroborated by philosophical reasoning. A thoroughgoing atheist, if he has a taste for the enterprise, might interpret religion in the light of his purely naturalistic categories. He might adopt a position similar to that of Fredrick Schleiermacher or Albrecht Ritschl and, no doubt, much of what he would have to say would be interesting even to the believer. From any view, religion is a human invention, even though its object is God. Although the question "Does God really exist?" is an important one, one need not solve that question to philosophically enquire about the nature of religion. The question of God's existence belongs to the sphere of metaphysics. Granted, how one settles that question will determine one's personal attitude toward religion.

To return to the distinction between the philosophy of religion and the psychology of religion, although the two are not the same, they are frequently confused largely because the same question, "Why is man religious?" can be answered from both perspectives. The philosopher may seek the logical grounding of the assent which leads to the practice of religion; the psychologist may investigate the feeling of awe in the presence of mystery and speak about the needs of the subject. Answers are determined by the way the question is put, and that in turn depends upon one's prior metaphysical analysis. If there is no evidence for the existence of God, the psychological question becomes why does the religious mind go beyond the confused signs of the world? What is the psychological movement which carries it beyond the evidence? As we shall see, a logical analysis of belief is one theory; a psychological analysis for it is another.

A philosophy of religion should in principle allow that the assent, which is belief, might, in fact, be rationally grounded. A philosophy of religion should not, at least immediately, rule out the possible rational foundation of belief. If it is closed to that possibility, then it cannot take religious faith seriously and must regard the believer as one who has failed to use sufficient intelligence or discretion in the placing of his commitments. If there is not at the outset of an inquiry the conviction that belief may be rationally grounded, then the contrary attitude will undoubtedly prevail, namely, that belief is not rational. If one begins with that supposition, then obviously religious belief stands in need of criticism in order that it may be replaced or revised in the interests of intelligent behavior. The social structures or institutions grounded on such beliefs, even though they may have benevolent effects, are on shaky intellectual ground and should be exposed as such.

Another problem endemic to the philosophy of religion is the difficulty of talking about religion in the abstract. A common denominator to all that is designated "religion" is difficult to discern, and even where such identification is attempted, the product is frequently vacuous if not meaningless. No author for long successfully talks about religion in a general way. Usually the focus quickly shifts to Western religions and then narrows further to Christianity and Judaism, with occasional references to Islam. Apart from the inability to keep all religious manifestations in mind, or the value of doing so, authors usually do not have a stake in religion in the abstract. But Western man has a stake in the major Western religious traditions. Because of the historical and continuing impact of his traditions, he must come to terms with them in a way in which he does not have to come to terms with religion more broadly defined.

With deliberation this book is called the *logic* of religion. It doesn't require extensive empirical investigation to notice a certain logic or structure to religion wherever it is found. This is particularly true of the Western religions on which this book focuses. One does not need a philosophical analysis of religion to recognize that religion is founded on certain beliefs or that religious belief is only one type of belief. A religious act of faith has much in common with other acts of faith. We accept most of what we know on the testimony of others. We believe that Paris is lovely in the spring, that there is such an entity as the DNA molecule which is responsible for inherited traits, that Michelangelo is the sculptor of *Moses*. Few physicists have actually performed the experiments upon which the inference to the existence of K and P mesons is based, yet all would agree that propositions enunciating their reality possess at least a high degree of probability.

Belief is usually rationally grounded in the sense that the believer has some reason for assenting, even when he has mistakenly assented. Conviction usually follows the presentation of evidence or testimony. That evidence or testimony has to be both consistent and in accord with what is already known. Some reports are customarily viewed with great suspicion, i.e., that of an automobile whose engine possesses an amazing ratio of efficiency, or another program for the eradication of poverty, or a fail-proof method for teaching mathematics. Sometimes the language used to report discoveries in the sciences is so metaphorical that we do not readily assent to the reality of "right-handed matter" or "anti-matter" or "drops of electricity." Our curiosity might be aroused by such reports, but we withhold assent. Similarly, with respect to reports from the social sciences which contravene common sense, we withhold assent.

So also in the domain of religious affirmation we instinctively distinguish. While we might be able to understand the impulse which leads certain primitive tribes to endow a fetish or the elements of nature with diverse properties and even appreciate the beauty of their rites, still we would be reluctant to regard their beliefs as well founded. In matters of religion, we tend to discriminate between primitive cults and the great religions of mankind. Certain religions present themselves as credible, and we can understand why an informed and intelligent person might subscribe to their tenets.

To return to a point made above, Western religion is founded on belief in a god or gods. A philosophical analysis of religion may appropriately begin with a study of the nature of the act of assent to certain principles or propositions, namely, that there is a God, that reality consists in more than spatio-temporal-physical and mental events, that history is guided and controlled by nonhuman forces, that individual existence does not terminate with the cessation of bodily processes. Assent can be generated by philosophical considerations or by a more-or-less gratuitous act of faith. By faith is meant a personal act of assent to propositions acknowledged to be true but for which there is no evidence, scientific or otherwise. Faith may entail hope or trust in a person or in an institution, but intellectual assent to some articulatible truth is primary. A religious act of faith, although similar to other acts of faith, differs in its object (God) and in the conviction that, for at least some of its propositions, no evidence is yet forthcoming. There can be a natural religion generated through philosophical considerations, but because philosophy is limited to a few, there are not likely to be the necessary numbers to create a community of philosophical theists. A community of believers is required not only for religion to exist but for it to maintain itself, develop, and exert a social and cultural influence.

There are other manifestations and implications of belief which should be noted at the outset before we examine the texts of any of the great thinkers proposed for consideration. Most of the philosophers chosen will in their own examinations bear out these prephilosophical observations. From the assent to God's existence, or with the recognition of a superior power which is in some fashion ultimately responsible for the course of natural events, certain things follow. Implied is a recognition of dependence and finiteness. An admission of dependence may lead to reverence and love. These attitudes will be expressed differently within different cultural contexts. The degree of sophistication in the intellectual tools utilized by the believer will determine the character of the belief and the resultant religion. Religious bodies arise as men attempt to worship collectively or to pay homage to the superior being. Most religions, however primitive, seem to include as essential features acts of worship, including the offering of sacrifice. Adoration and supplicative prayer are other acts of worship commonly found. Within revealed religions, such as Judaism, Christianity, and Islam, these common tendencies are more pronounced and are given a definitive form.

It is evident that any community which regards itself as the repository of certain truths regarding divine things must structure itself if it is to survive. Visible churches are the natural outcome of the religious community's attempt to perpetuate itself. The tasks which a religious community must undertake are many, but some are central.

One function which seems to be universally characteristic of religious bodies is that of worship. Worship is sometimes, but not always, bound up with sacrifice. In any case, a priesthood comes into being. Certain individuals are set apart who by public acts, example, and teaching show the way. They are the masters of rite. They lead the community of believers.

The definition, conservation, and development of doctrine are also important functions and are found analogously in all religious groups. There is need for a body of teachers who are selected for learning and holiness. The ecclesial body is of necessity an educator, and its leaders consequently are teachers, even where their primary function is the direction of worship. The bodily welfare of its members and of society at large is a concern of only some religious groups, primarily those which have arisen in the West. In the West, from biblical times religious groups have been concerned with the care of the sick, the homeless, the orphaned, the widowed.

Since worship requires ritual and suitable visible structures, the church may emerge as a patron of the arts. Equally as important as the development of doctrine is the development of appropriate ritual. Doctrine will develop through dialectic. The fortunes of doctrine, the province of theologians, will rise and fall with the state of

learning of the time. Theologians develop languages and method-
ologies, which can be plural in number while remaining faithful to
the basic deposit of faith. The community itself is the last authority on the essentials of the faith. A theology, or the language of
theologians, can be subjected to philosophical analysis. Religious
discourse can be submitted to analysis by means of formal logic
and semantics. One can ask, "What is the logical structure of faith?
The truth conditions of faith?"

Ritual, too, will have its guardians (priests) and creators (art-
ists). In the creation of ritual, the full scope of human inventive-
ness can be brought into play. Artifacts can be used minimally or
lavishly. Witness the difference between nineteenth-century American gothic and the grand baroque or rococo of seventeenth- and
eighteenth-century Spain. A matter of taste and culture.

Ritual necessarily uses many symbols—visual, spoken, and
written. To understand their meaning and significance, one must
enter the mind and heart of the religious person. In this context
philosophers must avoid taking the language or symbol out of
context. The combination of doctrine, ritual, and personal contemplation can create for the privacy of a few a "religious experience." But taken as a category or as an object of investigation, "religious experience" is vague and amorphous. One cannot start with
religious experience if one is to understand the religious mind. Too
much is presupposed. Religious symbols flow out of doctrine. It is
true that one doesn't have to assent to a given religion to appreciate the symbolic artifacts generated out of that religion and, similarly, one need not share a particular faith to contribute to the art
or literature of that faith. But to understand symbol, one must understand it within the set of beliefs which form its matrix. Symbols
include everything from words to incense and serve a variety of
purposes. There is a certain refinement in the use of symbols. The

ability to think analogically is said to be a mark of intelligence. The religious way of symbolizing, of celebrating, of marking passages or the seasons of the year is usually a very civil way and is similarly a mark of intelligence. Man loves pageantry, the occasion when the humdrum is replaced by splendor.

Given the variety of minds to be reached, many different symbols are likely to be employed. This reaching can be done beautifully or not. Religious symbolism at its best is represented by Bernini's *Colonnade* or Michelangelo's *David;* at its worst by a dashboard statue or dime store Buddha. Symbols can have many levels of meaning. A single crucifix can symbolize Christ's instrument of torture, His death, Christianity in general, one's faith commitment, and so on. So, too, the sacraments. Baudelaire wrote, and not without reason, "Priests are servants and secretaries of the imagination."

A further peril in taking religious experience as a point of departure is that there is nothing particularly religious in "feelings of contingency or dependence" or in the "awe felt upon the perception of the grandeur of the universe." Against those who take religion to be a natural sentiment it can be argued that man is not by nature religious, that religion, rather, is culturally induced. Religion may be "natural" in the sense that primitive and not-so-primitive man have in fact drawn the conclusion that human events are contingent upon the forces of nature and that behind those forces there is a mind which ought to be acknowledged in worship and placated by prayer and sacrifice. But such naturalness is grounded on inferences commonly made from judgments. If those judgments are not made, or the inference not drawn, the religious impulse will not follow.

This is a key question for exploration, i.e., whether religion stems from non-rational forces in man or whether man's intellec-

tual equipment leads him to acknowledge a fundamental dependence on a transcendent being. Those who seek to place religion on
a rational footing affirm either that reason is in some sense forced
to acknowledge a god or that belief makes sense even if God's existence cannot be demonstrated. Those who deny a rational ground,
while still acknowledging the naturalness of religion, place the origins of religion in man's emotional makeup. How one understands
the emotions is of obvious importance. Do the emotions follow
perception, or are they initiative of themselves? One's theory of religion is in some sense contingent upon one's theory of knowledge, imagination, and emotion.

It is assumed here that religion is more a matter of culture than
an innate disposition. On this view, religion is learned as everything else is learned. If divine revelation is denied and there is no
known evidence for affirming the existence of God, and this becomes culturally acknowledged, then religion should disappear.
Many would argue that this in fact is happening in the West. Feelings of finitude and dependence remain, but such are not to be
identified with religion. On the other hand, certain religions would
place those feelings in a larger context at least, and satisfy and encourage the believer precisely because of their explanatory value. If
one holds that emotion follows knowledge, then if I know that
there is a God, I will worship and I will order my life accordingly.
On such a view, I do not invent God because of a felt need for him.

GREEK AND ROMAN INSIGHTS
INTO THE NATURE OF RELIGION

Socrates, Plato, Aristotle, Cicero, Seneca

The Greek mind had a well-developed sense of "piety," piety in the sense that it disposed one to acknowledge debt, e.g., to one's parents, to one's country, and to the wellsprings of one's being.

Socrates (470–399 B.C.) was charged with impiety and thus corrupting the youth because he did not recognize his debt to the gods accepted by the state. Yet it is well known that Socrates was the enemy of neither morality nor the state, affirming as he did that the wise man is both good and happy. This doctrine has a bearing on the present topic, namely, man's attitude toward the divine. Socrates argued that happiness is integrated selfhood, an inner harmony of the self with itself, or put another way, personal integrity. This integrity is achieved through the formation of the will by insight. Insight itself is attained through "training," that is, through "purposeful thoughtfulness." Required is plain, hard, honest, humble thinking in the context of a triple dialogue with oneself, with others, and with the mysterious ultimate that lures man on. Virtue can be taught because the relevant insights can be communicated. The virtue of religion is a species of piety, the acknowledgment of one's debt to the gods, and it can be taught as any virtue is taught.

In *Euthyphro* Socrates discusses piety, which is that part of justice which concerns attention to the gods; the remaining part of justice concerns the service of men.[1] The virtue of justice binds all other virtues into a harmony and brings unity to the person as a whole. What does attention to the gods mean? The gods are not benefited or brought to a greater degree of perfection by anything that men do. The kind of attention Socrates has in mind involves a certain kind of service, a committing of oneself to a divine service. Prayer and sacrifice are modes of service. Such acts as honor, praise, and gratitude bring salvation to individuals, families, and states.[2]

On the subject of prayer, Xenophon (c. 430–356 B.C.) records that Socrates' ideal was "to pray for that which is good, without further specification, believing that the gods best know what is good."[3] In *Alcibiades II*, Plato (c. 428–348 B.C.) has Socrates approve this old Spartan prayer: "Give us, O king Zeus, what is good, whether we pray for it or not, and avert from us the evil, even if we pray for it."[4] Socrates' ideal of prayer is also shown in a beautiful prayer to Pan, which occurs at the end of the *Phaedrus:* "O beloved Pan, and all ye other gods of this place, grant to me that I be made beautiful in my soul within, and that all external possessions be in harmony with my inner man. May I consider the wise man rich; and may I have such wealth as only the self-restrained man can bear or endure." He then turns to Phaedrus and asks: "Do we need anything more, Phaedrus? For me that prayer is enough."[5]

1. Plato, *Euthyphro*, 12e. In *Dialogues of Plato*, 2 vols., translated by B. Jowett (New York: Random House, 1920).

2. Ibid., 14e.   3. Xenophon, *Memorabilia*, 1.3.2.
4. Plato, *Alcibaides II*, 143a.   5. Plato, *Phaedrus*, 279b.

Aristotle, in his day, will say that the word "father" when applied to Zeus includes the idea of his care for men. But this idea first appears in Greek literature in a passage of Plato's *Apology*, in which Socrates says to his judges that "no evil can come to a good man either in life or after death, and God does not neglect him."[6]

Plato followed Socrates in rejecting what he called the "indecent" fables told about the gods. In Plato's judgment, poets who make up such things are dangerous to the health of society. Plato's conception of the divine and of man's relation to the divine was most lofty. In the *Timaeus*, when Timaeus begins his story of "creation," we learn that the eternal model is the Demiurge himself:

Let me tell you then why the creator made this world of generation. He was good, and the good can never have any jealousy of anything. And being free from jealousy, he desired that all things should be as like himself as they could be.[7]

According to Plato the eternal being of the Demiurge is orderly. When he takes over discordantly moving primordial matter, he brings it from disorder to order. The eternal being of the Demiurge is also intelligent. Therefore, since intelligence cannot be present anywhere without dynamic soul *(psyche)*, the Demiurge fashions intelligence *(nous)* within the soul. We may say that he gives intelligence an in-soul embodiment. The Demiurge is also the symbol of "incarnation," the process of embodiment that bridges the gulf between eternal changeless being and time-and-space changeable becoming. This timeless model is brought down to earth and rendered incarnate in a multiplicity of things.

Clearly the Demiurge is not to be equated with Yahweh of the Hebrews; he is not experienced as utterly transcending his creation but as active within it. The Demiurge is pictured as an artist work-

---

6. Plato, *Apology*, 41b. In *Dialogues of Plato*, 2 vols., translated by B. Jowett (New York: Random House, 1920).
7. Plato, *Timaeus*, 30b.

ing with somewhat resistant materials that he has not made but that he struggles to shape in such a way that they express insofar as possible the goodness and the intelligibility of his model—the essential structure of his own being. The parallel between the Demiurge and human beings struggling to express in their existence the essentially good, orderly, intelligible structure of their selfhood is obvious.

Plato's philosophical outlook includes personal belief in the providence of higher intelligences with regard to human affairs. According to his pivotal philosophical conceptions, no city-state can attain a high degree of culture unless its rulers pattern it after the Ideal. As a matter of historical fact, Athens and other Greek city-states did reach a high and proud degree of civilization, yet some of their greatly revered leaders had not even heard of the Ideal, let alone received training in the doctrine. How account for their success? They ruled, says Plato, not by knowledge but by true opinions, which unfortunately are undependable and insecure because of the lack of any causal tie. The security and dependability of these opinions in the great Greek leaders required some cause apart from their own thinking, some inspiration from a higher type of intelligence than the merely human:

And therefore not by any wisdom, and not because they were wise, did Themistocles and those of whom Anytus spoke govern. . . . But if not by knowledge, the only alternative which remains is that statesmen must have guided states by right opinion, which is in politics what divination is in religion; for diviners and also prophets say many things truly, but they know not what they say. . . . Yes, and statesmen above all may be said to be divine and illumined, being inspired and possessed of God, in which condition they say many grand things, not knowing what they say.[8]

This notion is also present in a passage of the *Republic*, where Plato states that given the actual condition of human government

8. Plato, *Meno,* 99bd.

everywhere, based as it is upon traditionally received notions and not upon philosophical knowledge, the good that is present is due to a higher intervention: ". . . for I would not have you ignorant that, in the present evil state of governments, whatever is saved and comes to good is saved by the power of God, as we may truly say."[9] Plato believes that men so inspired, though few in number, are always to be found.

In the *Laws* Plato does not hesitate to propose legislation regarding religious observance. One magistrate at least will sacrifice daily to some god or demi-god on behalf of the city and citizens and their possessions.[10] In Book X of the *Laws* Plato lays down his proposals for the punishment of atheism and heresy.

To say that the universe is the product of the motions of corporeal elements, unendowed with intelligence, is atheism. "If you say that nature has bestowed the gifts of earth, you are merely giving a different name to God. For what is nature if not God and divine reason pervading the entire world and its parts? As often as you will you may find some different way to address the author of all that we have. You may call him 'Jupiter,' 'Supremely Good,' 'Supremely Great,' or by some other name."[11]

Plato argues that there must be a source of motion, and that ultimately we must admit a self-moving principle, called soul or mind, which is the ultimate source of cosmic movement. Plato decides that there must be more than one soul responsible for the universe because there is disorder and irregularity as well as order. There may be more than two. It is heresy to say that the gods are indifferent to men. The gods cannot lack the power to attend to small things. God cannot be too indolent or too fastidious to attend to details; even a human artificer attends to details. Provi-

9. Plato, *Republic*, VI, 492E–493A.   10. Plato, *Laws*, 828b.
11. Ibid., 899d.

dence does not involve interference with the laws of nature. Divine justice will at any rate be realized in the succession of lives.

According to Plato, a pernicious heresy is the opinion that the gods are venal and that they can be induced by bribes to condone injustice. As to the penalties to be inflicted on those proved guilty of atheism or heresy, Plato prescribes for a morally inoffensive heretic at least five years in a house of correction. A second conviction will be punished with death.

Heretics who exploit the superstition of others for their own profits or who establish immoral cults are to be imprisoned for life. No private shrines or private cults are to be permitted. However, before prosecuting an offender for impiety, the guardians of the law should determine whether the offense has been committed in earnest or from childish levity.[12] Although there is a difference in emphasis between the *Laws* and Plato's earlier works, his overall views are not different from those which he espoused in the much earlier *Republic*.

In the *Republic*, Plato says religion is beyond the sphere of the philosopher and the legislator; tradition is to be followed in these matters.

To Apollo, the god of Delphi, there remains the ordering of the greatest and noblest and chiefest thing of all. Which are they? he said. The institution of temples and sacrifices, and the entire service of the gods, demigods, and heroes; also the ordering of the repositories of the dead, and the rites which gave to be observed by him who would propitiate the inhabitants of the world below. These are matters of which we are ignorant ourselves, and as founders of a city we should be unwise in trusting them to any interpreter but our ancestral deity.[13]

---

12. Ibid., 909d.
13. Plato, *Republic*, IV, 427bc.

Unlike Plato, Aristotle (384–22 B.C.) provides no significant texts on the subject of religion, although in one place he offers a psychological explanation of the cause of belief in gods, namely, experience in dreams and the regular order and harmony in the universe. There is no doubt, however, that Aristotle argues to a number of concepts associated with the divine: to an immaterial order, to a first or ultimate cause which draws all things to itself, and to a self-thinking intellect, yet one would look in vain for texts in which he prescribes homage or piety.

Contrary to the lofty and spiritual philosophy of Plato is the analysis of the atomist Epicurus (341–270 B.C.), who taught that religion is a disease of the soul, having its origin in fear of the gods and the hereafter. Religion is not grounded in respect for the eternal law, as Socrates and Plato thought. Quite the opposite. The frightening qualities of nature lead men to search for the sources responsible for them. These sources can hardly be imagined as beneficent. Man has created his gods in part because he is convinced that evildoers will be punished in the hereafter. In this manner, man's evil conscience is at the root of religion.[14] Epicurus subscribed to a mechanistic or purely materialistic or atomistic interpretation of nature, not unlike that of Democritus.

Marcus Tullius Cicero (106–43 B.C.), lawyer, philosopher, statesman, and the greatest of Roman orators, regards social organization as closely related to the divine. In *De legibus* III he considers first the means by which the state should endeavor to win the favor of the gods, and second, the ways by which the state under divine favor should live and function.[15] In the one case, the state acts

---

14. Cf. *The Philosophy of Epicurus*, translated by George K. Strodach (1963).

15. Marcus Tullius Cicero (106–43 B.C.), *De legibus*, III. Influence of Cicero on Western thought is incalculable. For Aquinas he was the beloved and oft-quoted "Tully"; for the Renaissance, a major source. Cicero's *On the Commonwealth* and *On the Laws* were

through religious Deceremony and priestly order; in the other, through magistrates and groupings of the chief men and people.

He sets forth a code of religious laws, introduced by a preamble in which he urges all citizens of the ideal commonwealth to believe implicitly in the supremacy of the deathless gods. For the gods not only govern the universe, but they also perceive and record the acts and feelings of each individual. Accordingly, if reverence does not of itself inspire adoration, prudence will at least suggest the expediency of worshiping those beings who will be both witnesses against us and judges of our conduct.

Cicero draws up a set of religious prescriptions in legalistic terms. The gods must be approached reverently, in purity of heart, and without costly ceremonial. The manner in which men approach them should be both reverent and fitting. Although the law stresses purity of heart, it does not thereby imply that no importance is to be attached to purity of body. The body of a worshiper should be ceremonially clean. By forbidding costly ceremony, the law opens the rites of religion to all.

The divinities who are to be thus approached do not all possess identical significance. Cicero acknowledges a hierarchy among the gods.[16] In the first place come the gods of heaven; in the second, deified mortals such as Hercules and Aesculapius; next the personified abstractions such as intelligence, virtue, and faith; after these Cicero puts the dead, who are not to be considered as gods. Into this pantheon no new or imported gods will be admitted unless they have been officially accepted by the state. Citizens will not be allowed to worship the personification of any evil abstraction.

---

his first and most substantial attempts to adapt Greek theories of political life to the circumstances of the Roman Republic. Both display an indebtedness to Plato. *On the Commonwealth* and *On the Laws*, translation based on that of K. Ziegler and W. Goerler, edited by James E. G. Zetzel (Cambridge: Cambidge University Press, 1999).

16. Cicero, *De legibus,* II, 9.

Cicero further divides religious observance into urban and rural spheres. Certain practices are at all times forbidden. Women must not participate in nocturnal sacrifices except when duly performed on behalf of the people. No wicked person may offer gifts to the gods in the hope of softening their anger toward him. No one except attendants of the Great Mother of the Gods may collect money for religious purposes, and even they may do so only on the proper days. Cicero is convinced that the custom of taking money consumes property and disseminates superstition. No one may dedicate land that is the sacred possession of all the gods to any special purpose. Vows are to be strictly observed. Violations of the religious law will be punished. From those who are guilty of perjury, two penalties are exacted. Since, on the one hand, perjury is an offense against the gods, the punishment is death; and since, on the other hand, perjury intimately affects human life and interests, death is accompanied by disgrace.

In rural districts, where graves are the religious centers, the simple pieties of ancestral and family worship are to be carefully preserved. Recognizing the importance of religion in the countryside, he decrees days of relaxation, falling at such seasons of the year as naturally coincided with the end of the farmer's labor. In the cities, on the other hand, the gods are to be worshiped in temples, where statues bring them vividly before the eyes and thoughts of men. Among the ceremonial forms accompanying urban observance is that of public games.

Ritual is subject to the guidance of *sacerdotia* or public priests. Priests fall into distinct groups. The first that Cicero mentions are the *pontiff* who preside over all public and private ceremonies and supply information as to the proper form of all ritual. Within their competence also falls the duty of punishing with death any *vestal* who fails to keep her vow of chastity. Certain priests in this group are assigned to the worship of a particular divinity. These Cicero identifies as *flamens,* but their duties are not related.

Another class that Cicero identifies with sacral functions is the *vestals,* groups of women who direct the worship of Vesta. They guard the sacred fire, symbol of the city's domestic life, and may never allow it to become extinguished. Selected as young girls, *vestal* virgins are committed to thirty years of service.

A second group of priests are the *augurs.* They expound the will of Jupiter by the interpretation of signs and auspices. They are to determine, by appropriate ritual, whether the gods favor the state, its crops, and its officials. Their pronouncements, duly delivered after formal observation, are law to magistrates in the city and even to military commanders in the field. Mandates are to be enforced on penalty of death. The chief and pre-eminent power in the commonwealth is that associated with the authority of the *augurs.* Declaring war, concluding peace, or striking a treaty is done with the sanction of religion (the Fetial College). In Roman belief, political power, considered abstractly, flows from the gods. Human agents may properly exert political authority only when that authority is divinely sanctioned.

Seneca (c. 48 B.C.–65 A.D.), Rome's leading philosopher in the mid-first century A.D., in his treatise "On Private Life," raises the question: "What service to God is there in contemplation?" and he responds: "That the greatness of his work be not without witness."[17] Elsewhere he writes:

It is not by sacrificial victims, however fat and glittering with gold, that the gods are honored, but by uprightness and holiness of will in the wor-

---

17. Seneca, "On the Private Life," in *Moral and Political Essays,* edited and trans. by John M. Cooper and J. F. Procopé (Cambridge: Cambridge University Press, 1995), 175.

shiper. Good men with no more to offer than groats and meal-paste are devout, while the wicked cannot avoid impiety, however much they stain the altars with blood.[18]

Speaking of the value of prayer, he offers this insight:

Who ever says (that God does not grant favors) has closed his ears to the sound of prayer, of vows made in all places, in private and in public, with hands raised to heaven. This would not happen, I tell you, it could not be that nearly all mankind would have joined the lunacy of addressing deities that cannot hear and gods that cannot act, unless we had some knowledge of their favors toward us, of favors sometimes brought to us of their own accord, sometimes granted in answer to a prayer, of favors great and timely that free us from mighty threats by their coming.

His titles can be as many as his services to us. . . . Wherever you turn, you will find him coming to meet you. Nothing is void of him; he fills his own creation. You waste your time, most ungrateful of mortals if you say that you owe yourself not to God but to nature. You cannot have nature without God, nor God without nature. Each is the same as the other, differing only in function. . . . God confers on us the greatest and most important favors without any thought of return. He has no need for anything to be conferred, nor could we confer anything on him.[19]

18. Seneca, "On Favours," in ibid., 202.
19. Ibid., 276–80.

CHRISTIAN CONCEPTIONS OF BELIEF

Early Church Fathers, Augustine

With the advent of Christianity, Western thought underwent a dramatic shift. At the beginning of the Christian era there prevailed in Hellenistic philosophy the image of a universe imbued with reason and consequently shorn of mystery. The universe was regarded as intelligible, its design discernible by science and philosophy. With the teachings of Christ and the Apostles the cosmos of the Greeks took on new meaning.

Although Christianity was not introduced as a body of knowledge in opposition to Greek and Roman philosophy—that is, as one doctrine against another doctrine—its alternative character soon became apparent. In contrast to the thought of the Academy and the Lyceum, the natural, spontaneous form of Christianity was not written or didactic instruction. The Christian communities were initially made up of artisans, fishermen, and people of small means. While in Rome Stoic philosophers were lecturing to a relatively sophisticated audience and conducting a disinterested inquiry into nature; in Galilee Jesus was instructing uneducated people who knew nothing at all about Greek science or the Graeco-Roman conception of the world. The untutored people of Galilee could grasp parables and images more readily than the intricacies of dialectical argumentation. In the teaching of Christ and in that of the apostles, the world, nature, and society are presented not as objects of science but as inexhaustible reservoirs of images replete with spiritual significance—e.g., "the lily of the valley," "the prodigal son," "the lost sheep," and many others whose freshness and popular appeal contrast sharply with the conventional rhetoric and the studied eloquence of the Roman world. Christ teaches people how to attain happiness but not through the development of a Stoic will that treats all external events with indifference. Poverty, sorrow, wrongs, injustices, and persecutions are true evils but evils which, thanks to Christ's redemptive act, will be righted in the kingdom to come. Typical Christian teaching, such as joy in the midst of suffering in the expectation of eternal happiness, is quite different from the serenity of the Stoic who at each moment sees that moment in its entirety including its role in the fulfillment of his destiny.

From its beginnings in Galilee, Christianity spread rapidly from Jerusalem and Judea in the first century, particularly to the north and west, into Syria, Asia Minor, and to Rome. Beginning as a Jewish sect, appealing largely to Hellenized Jews, it first broadened its reach into the Gentile world largely through the efforts of the Apostle Paul. As it made fast its roots and grew, Christianity attracted converts from a wide social and intellectual spectrum. St. Paul is representative of highly educated Hellenized Judaism. One finds within his writings ample evidence of his familiarity with Greek philosophical thought, and he in part addressed hearers of like education.

Later when Christianity began to arouse the suspicion and hostility not merely of the Jews and political authorities but also of the pagan intellectuals, theoretical attacks on philosophical grounds had to be met with philosophical as well as theological arguments. Consequently among the writings of the Church Fathers and early apologists we find a pronounced philosophical element, largely Platonic but including elements of their limited knowledge of Aristotle and considerable knowledge of the Stoics. The teachings of Christ by implication introduce the problem of faith and reason. The originality of Christianity is seen from two distinct but perhaps complementary viewpoints. Some scholars call attention to the fact that Greek philosophy is essentially an objective representation of things and provides an image of the universe as an object for the contemplating mind. Aristotle taught that in knowing, the knowing subject becomes identical to its object. And in Stoicism, the moral subject has no freedom except in complete adhesion to its object. Without denying this, Christianity presents the specter of truly autonomous subjects, independent of the universe, who completely have a life of feeling and love that cannot always be translated into objective representation. In short, independent of the speculations of the Greeks concerning the cosmos, Christianity calls attention to the subjective, namely to the inner self, to the heart, to feeling, and to conscience.

The Greek world, in a manner of speaking, is a world without history. Its eternal order is not affected by time since it is either forever identical to itself or forever returning to the same point. On the Greek view, the history of humanity is a history of perpetual return of the same civilizations. The opposite idea that there is in the world radical change, absolute initiative, and veritable invention, is attributable to Christianity. Before Christianity overturned the cosmos of the Hellenes, the idea of historical progress would have been impossible. Distinctively Christian is the conception of a world created out of nothing. For the Christian, man has a destiny which is not thrust upon him from without but which he forges for himself through his obedience or disobedience to divine law. Christianity also teaches a new and foreseeable divine initiative to save men from sin, a ransom obtained through the suffering of the God-Man, Christ. These doctrines contribute to a dramatic new image of the universe. With Christianity we are no longer prisoners of fate; outcomes depend on the intimate, spiritual history of man and his relations with God. Man sees before him a possible future that, with the grace of God, he will enjoy in communion with God Himself. It is this trait that impressed the first pagans who concerned themselves seriously with Christianity. We may recall the complaint Celsus lodged against the Christians in a work entitled *The True Doctrine,* a work written near the end of the second century. He complains that Christians believe in a God who is not unchangeable since their God takes the initiative and makes new decisions in accordance with circumstances, that God is not impassive since He is affected by pity, and they believe in myths about Christ "which are not susceptible of allegorical interpretation."[1] They present their teaching as true history which cannot be reduced to a symbol or to a law of nature. For a Platonist like Celsus, Christianity has serious intellectual defects.

Thus we have pure Christianity fundamentally independent of Greek philosophical speculation ushering in an entirely new vision of the universe, a dramatic universe in which man is something other than a prisoner of nature. But things are to change. The distinctive teachings of Christ are received by those steeped in Hellenistic thought. They bring to those teachings the categories of Greece and Rome and recognize the implications of the Gospel. Attitudes with respect to philosophy on the part of the early Christian Fathers varied, but all affirmed that faith brings to man a higher idea of God and more perfect rules of human conduct than philosophy. The first major Christian apologist was Justin Martyr (100–165), of Greek descent who taught in the mid-decades of the second century. Justin studied Stoic, Aristotelian, Pythagorean,

---

1. Cf. Origen, *Contra Celsum,* translated by Henry Chadwick (Cambridge: Cambridge University Press, 195), 158.

and Platonic philosophy. He read Plato's *Apology, Crito, Phaedrus,* and *Phaedo* and concluded that philosophy leads to Christianity as its fulfillment. To Justin, Christianity appears as the best answer to questions raised by philosophers. The "rational," bequeathed by the Greeks, stands in need of "revelation." Here we find a philosopher finding in Christianity a philosophical satisfaction which he had not been able to find in Greek philosophy. Justin Martyr was convinced that Plato was superior to the Stoics in knowledge of God, though inferior to them in ethics. Each philosopher, seeing a portion of the Divine Word as related to his interest, gave expression to the Word, often an expression of extraordinary beauty. He rejected pagan polytheistic religion but welcomed such pagan philosophy as was consistent with biblical teaching.

The apologetic work begun by Justin was continued by "Athenagoros, Theophilus of Antioch, Clement of Alexandria, Origen, and others. All were familiar with Greek philosophy and esteemed portions of it, especially Platonic philosophy.[2]

One of Justin Martyr's disciples, Tatian (c. 120–73), was not so positive. Christians, he maintained, have been endowed by Revelation with a world-view immediately accessible to all and yet vastly superior to the philosophical conclusion of the Greeks. There is no need to study the Greeks as if they possessed the key to divine revelation. "Shun all heathen books," Tatian wrote. "Of what concern to you are strange ideas or laws or pseudo-prophets, which often lead inexperienced men into error. What is lacking to you in God's word, that you should turn to pagan nonsense."[3] Ter-

2. For an extended treatment of the Greek apologists and of early Christian speculation see Etienne Gilson, *History of Christian Philosophy in the Middle Ages* (New York: Random House, 1955), Part I–II, 9–66.

3. Tatian, *Didascalia et Constitutiones apostolosum*, Vol. VI, edited by F. X. Funk, Vol. I (Paterborn, 1905), 12, as quoted by David C. Lindberg "Science and the Early Church," in *God and Nature*, edited by Lindberg and Numbers (Berkeley: University of California Press, 1986), 24–25.

tullian (160–c. 240) adopted much the same view. "Wretched Aristotle," he wrote. "God has spoken to us; it is no longer necessary for us to philosophize. Revelation is all that is required. He who merely believes in the word of God knows more than the greatest philosophers have ever known concerning the only matter of vital importance."[4] In subsequent centuries St. Bernard and St. Peter Damicini (not to mention Martin Luther) would mirror this attitude. Today it can be found in Protestant fundamentalism and to some extent in Catholic theological circles. Like Tatian and for the very same reason, Tertullian died out of communion with the Church.

Another important thinker of the second century, Athenagoras (d. 180), saw certain problems and conclusions as common to philosophers and Christians. Although interested in Greek philosophy, he was not interested in it for its own sake. He did not condemn it, as did Tatian, but used it to further his own apologetics. The vague intimations of monotheism in Greek thought, he was convinced, do not compare with the clear-cut doctrine of Christianity. Still he held that philosophy opens one to the faith and confirms many of the truths contained within revelation.

Theophilus of Antioch (fl. 169), the sixth bishop of Antioch, attempted to define accurately the notion of creation *ex nihilo*, a notion not found in Greek philosophy. In an address to an opponent, Autolycus, he argued that God is not a maker or Demiurge but a creator. God is un-nameable and indescribable; all His names are borrowed either from His attributes or from His works, yet He can be known through His works.

Iranaeus (126–202), Bishop of Lyons wrote a treatise, *Against Heresies*, attacking the Gnostic who would substitute knowledge

---

4. Cf. Etienne Gilson, *History of Christian Philosophy in the Middle Ages* (New York: Random House, 1955), 44.

(gnosis) for faith *(pistis)*. He is not the first to write against the Gnostic but the first to show clearly the opposition of gnosticism to Christianity. Christianity, he proclaimed, is our own *gnosis*. In pointing out the inability of unaided reason to come to divine truths, he perhaps overstated his case. In attempting to destroy the Gnostics, he almost destroyed reason.

Among the early Church Fathers, Clement of Alexandria (D. C. 217) is important. He regarded Greek philosophy as absolutely essential for the defense of the faith against heresy and skepticism and for the development of Christian doctrine. He attempted to state the relationship of philosophy to theology. Clement construed his mission to be the teaching of the Christian Faith to the unbelievers rather than the defense of it against its opponents. Greek philosophy prepares the way and points to Christianity. Philosophy is a good and as such it is to be pursued, but nothing is required for salvation but faith. Yet faith has not replaced philosophy. Philosophy is useful to the Christian and may be properly called the handmaid of theology. Central to his teaching is the doctrine that truth is one.

The first task of the Christian is to eliminate from philosophy all that is false. In this, Christian wisdom acts as a selective principle which eliminates error and singles out truth in order to preserve it. The perfect Gnostic is one with the perfect Christian. The perfect philosophy is Christianity.

Clement undertook a systematic arrangement and defense of the moral and dogmatic teachings of the Church. Following Justin he maintained on the one hand that whatever is true in Greek philosophy is to be traced to the Divine Logos, "who enlighteneth every man who cometh into the world,"[5] and on the other hand

---

5. Cf. Etienne Gilson, *History of Christian Philosophy,* 29–34, for a discussion of Clement's understanding of Greek philosophy and its relation to faith.

that whatever errors are found in Greek philosophy must be attributed to man's weak and erring nature. The true *gnosis* is not the alleged esoteric doctrine of Christ, but the teaching found in the Gospels and in the Church which Christ founded. He who assents to the teaching of Christ and His Church, without the aid of philosophy as an intellectual basis, possesses faith, but he does not possess *gnosis,* which is to faith what the full grown man is to the child. Just as the Stoics idealized the wise man, Clement set up the Christian Gnostic as the idealized type of Christian.

Origen of Alexandria (185–c. 254), an Egyptian, is considered one of the great names in the history of Christian thought despite his many theological errors from an orthodox Christian viewpoint. A prolific writer, sometimes called a universal genius, he became a Christian biblical exegete worthy of translation by St. Jerome. Origen possessed an extensive knowledge of Greek philosophy—Aristotelian, Platonic, Stoic, and Epicurean. He adopted the basic elements of Plato's cosmology and psychology while borrowing his terminology and definitions from Aristotle. One of his students said of him: "He required us to study philosophy by reading all existing writings of the ancients, both philosophers and religious poets, taking care not to put aside or reject any . . . apart from the writings of atheists. . . . He selected everything that was true in each philosopher and set it before us, but condemned what was false."[6] In Origen's judgment, Greek philosophy is neither good nor bad; it can become either according to the use made of it. For the Christian, Scripture is the starting point, but the Bible needs to be understood. There is always a literal sense, but there is also an allegorical sense. Its anthropomorphism is not to be taken at face value. When the words of the Bible suggest something im-

---

6. Gregory Thaumaturgus in *Origenem oratio,* quoted by M. L. Clarke, *Higher Education in the Ancient World* (London: Routledge & Kegan Paul, 1971), 126–27.

possible, they must be understood in an allegorical fashion. True philosophy is needed to understand and properly implement this distinction. This view of the melding of philosophy with Scripture was also to be taken by St. Augustine, beyond dispute the greatest figure of this period.

St. Augustine (354–430) stands at the watershed of two worlds and may be considered a bridge between classical philosophy and Christianity.[7] The old world was passing away; the new world was coming into being. His major works, *The City of God* and *Confessions,* are Christian classics, read in every generation since his time. Augustine wrote commentaries on the Old and New Testaments and produced works such as *On the Teacher, Free Will,* and *Nature of Belief.* His works reveal a man broadly educated in the full range of the liberal arts. In his *Retractations* he reports that he once intended to write manuals on all the liberal arts, including arithmetic, geometry, music, and the elements of philosophy.

The Neoplatonic influence on Augustine is no more evident than in his reading of the text in which God reveals Himself to Moses as "I Am Who Am," a text that leads Augustine to conceive of God in the language of Being, that is, as the One of Plotinus. God is eternal and immutable as contrasted with the temporality and mutability of things. God created the world out of pure love. God spoke, and since His word was both His will and His power, the world was. The world was created *ex nihilo,* presupposing only the existence of God. All that God wills is good. Augustine's con-

---

7. *The City of God,* written between 413 and 426, is universally regarded as Augustine's greatest work. For an English translation from the critical edition of B. Domsart and A. Kalb, see R. W. Dyson, *The City of God against the Pagans* (Cambridge: Cambridge University Press, 1998). For an overview of his philosophy, see Etienne Gilson, *The Christian Philosophy of Saint Augustine* (New York: Random House, 1960), and Frederick Copelston, *A History of Philosophy,* Vol. II: *Medieval Philosophy: Augustine to Scotus* (Westminster, MD: The Newman Press).

ception of God leads him to affirm that God created all things at once. World history is but a progressive unfolding. Like Origen he affirms that the account of *Genesis* is but a metaphor.

Greatly influenced by Plato, Augustine affirmed that created things participate in the divine ideas; they are imitations of their models in the divine intellect. There is in nature a hierarchy of being. Each and every one to some extent reflects the perfection of divine being. Augustine's doctrine of immateriality pervades the whole of his philosophy and is especially pronounced in his theory of knowledge, but that is outside the scope of this enquiry. On the subject of participation, St. Thomas also is manifestly indebted to Plato.

Augustine had much to say about the moral order. There is a moral illumination comparable to a scientific illumination by which we come to know the principles of the natural law. But knowing what is right is not the same as doing what is right. Man is not only intellect but also will. The will must place itself in accord with the dictates of reason. The moral life is difficult. As a result of the fall, the body rebels against reason, resulting in concupiscence and ignorance. Instead of controlling the body, the soul is often controlled by it. The Fall of man was not necessary, but from the beginning it was possible. Though he fell by his own free will, his free will is not sufficient to raise him up again. Grace is required. The Fall was a movement of cupidity; the return is a movement of love.

Christians are best equipped to make the return journey, given that both knowledge and grace are available to them. Christians are temporally united by a common love. But besides being members of an earthly city, Christians are members of an eternal city. Natural knowledge is to be sought not for its own sake. We are to set our hearts on things celestial and eternal rather than earthly and temporal. Augustine acknowledged the utility of natural knowledge for the elucidation of Christian doctrine and the exegesis of Sacred Scripture. Indeed, elements of Greek natural philosophy are to be found throughout his works. Yet Augustine maintained there is no cause for alarm if the Christian "should be ignorant of the force and number of the elements. It is enough for the Christian to believe that the only cause of created things is the goodness of the creator."[8]

Yet Augustine writes "with regard to the obscurities of natural things which we know were made by the omnipotent God, the Creator, we should make an investigation, not by affirming, but by inquiring."[9]

8. *Euchiridion,* translated by Albert C. Outler in *Library of Christian Classics* (Philadelphia: Westminster Press, 1955) Vol. 7, 341–42.

9. Augustine, *On Genesis: Against the Manichees and on the Literal Interpretation of Genesis: An Unfinished Book,* translated by Roland Teske, S. J. (Washington DC: The Catholic University of America Press, 1991), 43.

THE RELATION OF FAITH TO REASON IN
AQUINAS AND THE REFORMERS

Aquinas, Luther, Calvin

St. Thomas Aquinas (1224–74) is regarded as the greatest of medieval theologians, and the study of his philosophy has been recommended by every pope since his death. It was specifically endorsed by Leo XIII in his encyclical *Aeternae Patris* (1879), which enjoined the Catholic world to study Thomas as an antidote to the secular and atheistic philosophies of his day. Thomas is studied by both theologians and philosophers. His commentaries on the works of Aristotle remain among the most authoritative ever written.

Thomas brought to his study of the Catholic faith not only Plato, the Neoplatonists, the Stoics, and the teachings utilized by Augustine but Augustine himself, whom he quotes more than any other philosopher. In addition to those sources, he had access to important works of Aristotle unavailable to his Latin predecessors. His *Summa Theologiae,* written as a handbook for contemporary use, begins by setting out what can be known of God by natural reason and then develops that knowledge with the aid of Sacred Scripture into a theological masterpiece that has been studied in every generation since. The relation of reason to faith is clearly explicated in a manner that serves as a benchmark for many contemporary studies. Our interest in Thomas is not merely antiquarian. He provides for the modern reader a viable understanding of the nature of religion that can take its place among contemporary treatises.

St. Thomas does not have a self-contained or explicit treatise on the subject of religion. Nevertheless, to anyone familiar with his writing, it is evident that his work not only presupposes a theory of religion but articulates one on a piecemeal basis within the context of other discussions. To put the pieces together is to have a philosophy of religion which can speak to numerous issues raised within the discipline as it is practiced today. This is not to say that Thomas has anticipated every contemporary concern. There are obviously many issues he did not address, some provided by the history of Western religion and some resulting from precisions in philosophy itself. Thomas, as any other medieval, modern, or contemporary thinker, might be open to the charge of limited acquaintance with religion globally considered. An examination of the source material available to Thomas would disclose that he was aware of the religious outlook of the Hebrews and that he knew something of Islamic creeds and practices. He was not aware of the tribal religions in Africa or of the major religions of Asia.[1] In that respect he is not impoverished by eighteenth-century standards. It can be shown that even the most widely acknowledged philosophers of religion in the twentieth-century focus on little else other than Western religion. It may also be argued that anthropological

---

1. R. Southern, in his *Western Understanding of Islam*, argues that the West as a whole knew little of Islam in the thirteenth century, as distinct from knowledge of Islamic philosophical thinking. See his interesting discussion of Roger Bacon's knowledge of Islamic philosophy and his failure to realize that this was not the same as orthodox Islamic theology and religious belief, p. 60.

studies of primitive religion add little to the data relevant to the philosophy of religion. One is less apt to understand religion when attention is fixed on its lower forms or on primitive superstitions than when study is directed to its higher manifestations, just as one is apt to learn more about painting in the Uffizi Gallery than by studying the artistic creations of children. Primitive forms are important in studying the evolution of religion, but chronological development is not to be confused with the structure of the object. In the order of time the imperfect may precede the perfect, but in the natural order the perfect is more revealing than the imperfect. It is no more necessary to have an exhaustive knowledge of the imperfect forms of religion in order to reflect upon the nature of religion than it is necessary to know the history of natural philosophy in order to understand quantum mechanics.

Thomas's basic insights with respect to religion may be said to be classical and to differ in little respect from those of Cicero or Seneca. The continuity is seen in the sources Thomas employs, principally Cicero, Seneca, and Macrobius. Thomas's theory of religion is classical in the sense that he treats religion as a moral virtue, that is, as a species of justice. Thomas accepts Cicero's judgment, expressed in De legibus, "[there is] no nation or tribe so uncultured that it does not acknowledge some sort of deity," and, consequently, none without worship; this is an expression of acknowledged dependence upon God, a judgment frequently repeated by Thomas.[2]

For Thomas, to acknowledge God's existence and man's dependence upon Him is to recognize a debt. The formal acknowledgment of any indebtedness, whether it be to parents, nation, or God, is an act of piety. Man pays his debt through acts of piety and

---

2. The primary text for Thomas's treatment of religion is the *Summa Theologiae* II–II, q. 81, aa. 1–8.

in the case of God through worship.[3] Before developing this theme, it should be noted that in other passages Thomas discusses religion from at least two other points of view. One is etymological, the other is from the standpoint of the common usage of the term. In both the *Summa Theologiae* and the *Summa Contra Gentiles,* he discusses the origin of the term itself.[4] Augustine, he says, found the origin of the word *religio* in the verb *re eligere* (to re-elect), Cicero in the verb *re legit* (to ponder over, to read again), and Lactantius in the verb *re ligare* (to bind back).[5] Thomas discusses all three views without dismissing any, although in a number of passages he seems to favor the last, which more directly connotes the bond which he takes to be the heart of religion. That binding of man to God, says Thomas, flows from several sources. Because God is a being of infinite excellence and worth, man owes Him reverence; because God is his creator and the source of all that he possesses, man owes Him service; and because God is man's last end, man owes Him love. A third approach is found in other passages when Thomas distinguishes among common usages of the word, noting that the term may designate a moral virtue, a social institution, or a state of life. These several approaches to an understanding of religion are not incompatible.[6]

Though in the *Summa Theologiae* Thomas begins his treatment of religion as a species of justice, his philosophy of religion can be said to begin with an analysis of the nature of the act of assent to the fundamental principles upon which religion is grounded —namely, that there is a God, that reality consists in more than spatio-temporal-physical and mental events, that history is guided and controlled by a nonhuman force, and that individual existence

---

3. Thomas's most extended treatment of worship is found in the *Summa Theologiae* when he is discussing the moral and ceremonial precepts of the old law, I–II, q. 100ff.

4. *Summa Theologiae,* II–II, q. 81, a.1.   5. Ibid.

6. Ibid.

does not terminate with the cessation of bodily processes. Assent to those principles can be generated by philosophical considerations or by a more-or-less gratuitous act of faith. Faith is then defined as a personal act of assent to propositions acknowledged to be true but for which there is not sufficient scientific or philosophical evidence.[7] Faith may also entail hope or trust in a person or institution, but intellectual assent to some articulated truth is primary. Religious faith, although similar to other kinds of faith, differs in its object (God) and in the conviction that for at least some of its propositions, sufficient evidence is not available. Essential to belief and especially religious belief for Thomas is the acceptance of something as true on the authority of another. Without this there would be no motive for assent. In the case of religious belief this other is God.

In the *de Veritate* Thomas develops his interesting analysis of the nature of faith.[8] Belief, he says, resides in the judgment act of the intellect, not in simple apprehension. We believe or disbelieve true or false statements. The mind, he says, may be compared to primary matter, which is indeterminate of itself and potential to all physical forms. Left to itself, the mind is able to receive all intelligible objects and is no more determined to a positive statement about any topic than to a negative statement. This indifference disappears when the intellect is moved by a factor other than itself to one or the other alternative. This movement can come from its own proper object, namely, an evident truth, or from the will, which commands. Faced with a "yea" or a "nay," the receptive mind can be affected in various ways. If it is swayed to neither side, it remains in a state of doubt. If it tends to one side rather than the other, yet without being entirely committed, it is in a state of opin-

---

7. For an extended treatment of the act of faith, see *Summa Theologiae,* II–II, q. 2, aa. 1–10.

8. *Summa Theologiae,* q. 14, 1.

ion. Faced by evidence, either immediate (first principles) or mediate (demonstration), it is in possession of certain or scientific knowledge. Short of conclusive evidence, the intellect may adhere to one side or the other but only because the will enters into the decision. Evidence that is insufficient to require the intellect to assent is nonetheless capable of moving the will. For example, one person takes the word of another for the sake of decency and common sense. In the case of belief, the intellect does not arrive at an object through its own proper motion, namely, coming to see the incontrovertible truth; instead its assent is motivated by factors affecting the will.

Though faith entails a worldview and Thomas can echo Augustine's *"credo ut intelligam,"* it is not this advantage which motivates or prompts belief. Between a natural worldview and the worldview provided by faith, there is a continuum. What is known through faith complements and perfects what is known through experience and reason. Belief for Thomas is not the satisfaction of a psychological need, nor does it involve a dramatic shift in perspective, as if a darkened intellect suddenly comes into light. A natural knowledge of nature has opened the way for beliefs which reinforce and supplement reason. New things are seen, but they are not startling; they were merely inaccessible. Later the positions of Luther and Calvin will differ considerably from that of Thomas. Both reformers will so emphasize the effect of the Fall on human intellect that faith becomes a gratuitous leap into the unknown.

For Thomas, assent is more closely analogous to a decision than to a blind leap. Reasonable assent is preceded by the process of wondering and weighing of evidence in which alternatives are considered. During the preliminary stage of wondering or questioning, we sit on the fence in a state of suspended judgment. The evidence is inconclusive. Eventually we may come off the fence on one side, accepting one alternative and rejecting others. The preferential character of assent is unavoidable. We cannot believe without also disbelieving. If we accept one proposition, we reject its negation. Assent is the taking of an attitude toward an entertained proposition. With respect to divine revelation, reason either admits or denies its possibility. If it sees the possibility of revelation and is further convinced that revelation has taken place, the person so convinced is morally bound to accept that revelation. If he doubts the existence of revelation, he is obligated to inquire further. Until he has made the inquiry, he cannot plead invincible ignorance. Once undertaken, his inquiry will either lead him to certitude or leave him in doubt. If it leads to certitude, then he must obey a certain conscience.

Thomas does not deny that there can be a natural religion generated through philosophical considerations, but because philosophy is limited to a few, there are not likely to be the necessary numbers to create a community of philosophical theists. A community of believers is required for religion to exist. Visible structures themselves are the natural outcome of the religious community's attempt to perpetuate itself.[9]

Thomas is aware that expressions of the reverence and love which follow from an acknowledgment of God's existence will be given different forms within different geographic regions. The degree of sophistication in the intellectual tools utilized by the believer will determine the character of the belief and the resultant religion. But all religions, no matter how primitive, entail as an essential feature acts of worship, including the offering of sacrifice. Adoration and supplicative prayer are other acts of worship that follow belief. Though Thomas does not offer any justification for the assertion, he declares, "At all times and among all nations, there

9. *Summa Theologiae*, II–II, q. 4, a. 2.

has always been the offering of sacrifices."[10] In any case, a priest-hood is a concomitant feature of religion. Priests so conceived are men set apart who by public acts, example, and teaching show the way; they are the masters of rite; they lead the community of believers.

The definition, conservation, and development of doctrine is an important function of the religious body and is analogously found in all religious groups. Consequently there is need for an order of teachers who, by virtue of their office, are selected for wisdom and uprightness. The religious community of necessity becomes an educator, and its leaders are consequently teachers, even where their primary function is the direction of worship. Doctrine will develop, as the Fathers well understood, through dialectic. Thomas has no doubt that theology is a science capable of demonstration from principles. Yet for him the community itself is the last authority on the essentials of the faith.[11]

Since worship requires bodily as well as mental activity, the development of appropriate ritual is almost as important as the development of doctrine. Thomas acknowledges existing variations in modes of worship. He takes it for granted that methods of worship are a proper subject of ecclesial regulation and that laws governing worship will vary from one community to another. But no community can avoid the use of sensory aids. Man's very nature requires the use of artifacts to lead the mind to things divine. Artifacts may be used minimally or lavishly. How they are employed is a matter of taste or culture.[12] In ritual, of necessity, many symbols,

10. *Summa Theologiae*, II–II, q. 85, a. 1.
11. *Summa Theologiae*, I, q. 1, a. 2.
12. *Summa Theologiae*, I–II, q. 101; II–II, q. 87, a. 7; also *Summa Contra Gentiles*, Bk. III, chap. 119. Theology as a science demonstrates conclusions from principles, at least one of which is accepted on faith and is not demonstrated philosophically or discovered naturally.

visual, spoken, and written, are employed. Their meaning or significance is derived from the purpose for which they are utilized, the insights they are meant to convey. Many contemporary philosophers could learn from Aquinas the need to view language and symbol within context. The logic of Aquinas's approach forces one to recognize that religious symbols flow out of doctrine. One does not have to be of a given religion to appreciate the artifacts generated out of that religion, and similarly one need not share a particular faith to contribute to the art or literature of that faith; but to understand symbol, one must understand it within the set of beliefs which form its matrix, an understanding which can only come with intimate acquaintance. Given the variety of minds grappling for expression and the multiplicity of inspirational purposes to be achieved, it is not surprising to find in religious symbols a richness unsurpassed in any other area of life. Following Aquinas, we can say that the religious way of symbolizing, of celebrating, or making passage of the seasons of the year is usually a very civil way. Man loves pageantry, the occasion when the humdrum is replaced by splendor.

There are obviously degrees of refinement in the use of symbols. Some are relatively simple and straightforward; others, because of their subtlety, require considerable intelligence and learning. Symbols can have levels of meaning, as Augustine suggested with respect to Sacred Scripture. Historically considered, the level of artistic achievement reached in Thomas's own period was one of the highest the world has known, but Thomas makes no mention of contemporary art forms.

A question often raised within the context of present-day philosophy of religion is whether religion stems from non-rational forces in man or whether man's intellectual equipment leads him to acknowledge a fundamental dependence on a transcendent being. As we shall see, this is Hume's way of raising the question, and his approach was to have considerable influence on nineteenth-century philosophy. Those who affirm the reasonableness of religion affirm either that reason is in some sense forced to acknowledge a God or that belief makes sense even if God's existence cannot be demonstrated. Those who deny a rational ground, while still acknowledging the naturalness of religion, place the origins of religion in man's emotional makeup. How one understands the emotions is of obvious importance. Do the emotions follow perception, or are they initiative of themselves? Thomas's answer is clear-cut, but beginning with David Hume we find an entirely different account which finds its most forceful expression in Freud.

For Aquinas religion is more a matter of culture than of innate disposition.[13] Given his approach, there is nothing particularly religious in "feelings of contingency or dependence" or in the "awe felt upon the perception of the grandeur of the universe." Religion may be "natural" in the sense that primitive and not-so-primitive man have in fact concluded that human events are contingent upon the forces of nature and that behind those forces there is a mind which ought to be acknowledged in worship and by prayer and sacrifice. But such naturalness is grounded in inferences commonly made from judgments. If those judgments are not made or the inference not drawn, the religious impulse will not follow. In Thomas's view, religion is learned as everything else is learned. If divine revelation is denied and there is no known evidence for affirming the existence of God, and this becomes culturally acknowledged, then religion should disappear. Feelings of finitude and dependence remain, but such cannot be identified with religion, though religion would place those feelings in a larger context. Christianity, at least, satisfies and encourages precisely because of its explanatory value. If one holds that emotion follows

13. Cf. *Summa Contra Gentiles*, Bk. III, chap. 120.

knowledge, then if I know there is a God, I will worship and I will order my life accordingly. On such a view, I do not invent God because of a felt need for him.

There are many other issues normally addressed by the philosophy of religion to which Thomas could speak. Thomas would not confuse morality with religion or spend much time arguing the possibility of morality apart from religion. His moral law doctrine clearly places morality in the natural domain. Reason is able to discern a natural order to which human action must conform if men are to perfect themselves. The religious mind is not confined to the endorsement of secular morality. Morality in many respects is changed within a religious context. Suffering and death take on a meaning they do not have in a purely naturalistic context. Similarly, an ascetic life of renunciation or one of sacrifice acquires a value it would not have within a purely naturalistic order. A conception of God as personal and loving has implications; prayer and contemplation only then become habits of mind to be recommended. In the face of adversity, a religious outlook can inspire hope, holding out a promise of eternal reward for actions that bear no temporal fruit. Christianity counsels patience, love, understanding, long suffering, and humility. Some, but not all of these, conflict with a purely secular outlook. Thomas maintains that although basic moral principles are discernible by unaided reason, it is fitting that because of their importance they be revealed by God since the content of revelation is accessible to all mankind, whereas philosophy is not.

With respect to the social and cultural value of religion, Thomas is not without insight. That the state has a stake in the unity of religion had long been recognized in the West. As we have seen, Cicero and Seneca, because they were convinced of the importance of religion to the state, thought it necessary for the state both to promote and to regulate religious observance. Thomas is also aware of Ambrose's treatise on the relation between Church and state. Thomas's own position emphasizes the common good as a norm against which assessments are to be made. The civic and religious orders are distinct, each having separate but complementary functions. In a proper relationship, there should be no conflict but mutually supportive activity. The beneficent effect of a single worshiping community is not to be denied, but it is not an end to be sought. The authentic teachings of Christ are to be made known, and in its teaching function the Church may well be assisted by the state, but the Church is not properly conceived as an instrument for the attainment of state objectives.

To develop this topic further would carry us too far from our primary purpose. These reflections are intended to show that Thomas, while not the author of a specific philosophical treatise on the structure and value of religion, does nevertheless have much to say on many topics which are normally discussed in the philosophy of religion. He can tell us what religion is and does, the nature of belief, and the function of a religious community. He understands the role of symbol and the importance of rites. A danger may lie in having him speak to too many contemporary concerns and thus to force his speech.

The Protestant Reformation and the consequent dividing of Christianity in the early sixteenth century raises anew the relationship between faith and reason. The conflict between the Reformers and Rome was not merely a theological dispute but reflected a deep cultural fissure—nothing less than the repudiation of an intellectual tradition. The social and political changes that followed the Reformation may have been more the work of political and military opportunists than of ecclesiastical authorities. Yet the ground for a major cultural shift had been laid in the intellectual order as the older scholasticism gave way to a new humanism. The common understanding respecting the sources of Christianity and its doctrinal development from Apostolic times were redefined by Luther and Calvin as they advanced a radical understanding of the Fall, sin, grace, faith, salvation, and the nature of the priesthood. Lost was the Graeco-Roman confidence in the intellect characteristic of medieval scholasticism. Scholastic discourse was displaced by personal meditation as the only reliable guide to the Sacred Scriptures, and as such need not be mediated by authority.

According to Martin Luther (1483–1546), all men are in possession of some natural knowledge of God's existence. This knowledge is an inborn truth of the human mind. Although the natural mind can know that God exists, it cannot determine with certainty who or what God is in His own nature. As a consequence of the Fall, our intellectual power is darkened and rendered impotent in matters involving the divine perfections. Luther's low assessment of reason may have had a primarily religious origin. He feared that metaphysics of the schoolmen might be taken as the foundation of faith and thus deprive faith of its gratuitous and independent nature, a key component of his doctrine of will.

Philosophical reflection had little or no relevance to theology or to an understanding of Christian belief for Luther, and the same can be said of John Calvin, a French theologian and ecclesiastical statesman (1509–64). Classical learning and the metaphysics of the Schoolmen were no substitute for personal faith and interiority. Reason, they argued, should be devoted to the promotion of the social good and individual temporal happiness, not to abstract speculation. Rejecting Aristotle's view of nature, Luther also rejected the use of Aristotle's *Ethics* in theories of salvation.[14] In the

---

14. *Luther's Works*, edited by Jaroslav Pelican and Helmut T. Lehman, 56 vols. (Philadelphia: Muhlenberg Press, 1955), Vol. 26, 127.

Ethics, Aristotle taught that a person had the innate capacity to lead a virtuous life but did not acquire virtue without effort and practice. Aquinas in speaking of grace claimed that active moral cooperation in a state of grace led to righteousness and enabled the person to grow closer to God. On the view of Aquinas, grace perfects nature, cultivating the human capacity for virtue inherent in human nature.

Luther, as a result of his belief in the radical sovereignty of God, adopted the opposite view. Human nature, Luther taught, cannot be improved by virtuous actions, at least not in any way important for salvation. Luther flatly asserted, "Virtually the entire *Ethics* of Aristotle is the worst enemy of grace."[15] Luther denied that powers inhering in the nature of a thing control its behavior and purpose. Whereas Aristotle and Aquinas understood purposive change as the fulfillment of what exists potentially, Luther denied that the potential of a thing determines its fulfillment because only God controls its behavior and purpose. Depending on His purpose, God may command natural things such as water, wind, or trees to behave according to their natures or against them. God, being the only source of grace and salvation in the spiritual world, is similarly the sole origin of motion and activity in nature. Having rejected Aristotle's view of nature as possessing intrinsic powers, Luther, with consistency, affirmed that God is the only active power in human "justification." Nature has no power of its own.

Because of its overzealous attempt to reconcile faith with reason, the Catholic Church failed to understand the substance of the spiritual domain, which is the centrality of grace in the economy of salvation. The Church in abusing reason obscured faith. Christ, not reason, is salvific. But the Christ who is encountered as an object of knowledge can be of no assistance to the troubled conscience; this is not the Christ of faith. The chasm between knowing

15. Ibid.

about Christ and *knowing* Christ is immense. Christ must be discovered as effectual within us.

John Calvin, in his *Institutes of the Christian Religion,* similarly developed a theory of knowledge.[16] True wisdom, he maintained, consists of knowledge of God and ourselves. How do we acquire knowledge of God? Fallen man can apprehend the divine nature with the aid of Scripture. But first Calvin makes a distinction: God the Creator can be approached in two ways; through natural reason and through Sacred Scripture. God the Redeemer is known only through Sacred Scripture. Though God the Creator can be approached in two ways, He is known only by supernatural faith. Natural reason is not superfluous, but it is intrinsically dependent on the guidance of the Bible. The divine essence is forever hidden and inaccessible to us. No proportion can be established between the human nature and the divine nature.

Like Luther, Calvin maintained that the human mind, due to a natural impulse, spontaneously affirms the existence of God as the one maker of the world, distinct from the works of His power, and that He demands the service of our worship. Calvin then raised the decisive question of whether our human mind can discern the general marks of God's character from the mind's experience of the world. He insisted that no answer can be given without adverting to the Fall of man, which the pagan philosophers did not know and which the Catholic schoolmen did not correctly interpret. With the Fall, man's intelligence was not annihilated, but it was corrupted to the point where its feeble sparks of instinctive knowledge of God were all but extinguished. Man, in his depraved condition, is thus unable to clearly discern the divine features in the mirror of nature.

A philosophy of God is *not* impossible by reason of God's

16. John Calvin, *Institutes of the Christian Religion,* translated by Henry Beveridge, 2 vols. (London: Clarke, 1953).

infinity or by reason of man's finitude; it is impossible by reason of historical man's sinfulness. Although a natural knowledge of God is impossible, this does not mean that fallen man ceases to search after evidence of God in the world or that he is fully aware of his predicament. As a result of revelation, Holy Scripture supplies us with the indispensable spectacles for looking into the mirror of the world and for seeing aspects of the divine nature about which the world remains silent. The true and right knowledge of God involves a formal submission to revelation and to the Christian mode of worshiping God. Anything falling short of this norm is likely to be a confused, transient, and error-ridden glimpse.

Calvin maintains that philosophical reasoning about God must result in contradictory and idolatrous views, not because he has studied the history of philosophy but because his theological doctrines of the Fall and biblical faith require it. Natural reason is corrupted reason and is therefore unreliable reason.

A generation later we find another dissident taking the opposite stance, Giordano Bruno (1548–1600), who is often regarded as a link between Renaissance humanism and the modern scientific era. In his chief work, *Concerning the Cause, Principle, and One* (1584),[17] Bruno maintains that philosophy alone contains a clear, explicit knowledge about God, man, and nature. Three epistemological canons undergird his position. Those who seek a natural knowledge of God must be sufficiently reflective to distinguish between opinions received through a supernatural faith and those based on the evidence of nature. Furthermore, they must have courage to criticize famous philosophical authorities.

Bruno's philosophy of God follows his theory of substance. The capital difference between a theologian and a philosopher is that the latter recognizes no transcendent creator or first principle

---

17. Giordano Bruno, *Concerning the Cause, Principle, and One,* translated in S. Greenberg, *The Infinite in Giordano Bruno* (New York: King's Crown Press, 1950).

which is distinct in being from the universe itself. God is substantially one with nature. Thus we can say with confidence that God is revealed in nature.

Bruno's gnosticism was to have less direct effect on future generations than the ideas of Luther and Calvin. We find Luther amply reflected in Kierkegaard and, of course, in the Evangelical Christianity that he inspired with his emphasis on Scripture and on its private interpretation to the exclusion of a hierarchically organized teaching church. Whereas Aquinas will say that God is being itself and nothing else, Luther would direct our attention to the person of Jesus Christ.

The lasting difference between Aquinas and the Reformers is graphically illustrated by the different seminary curricula of Catholic educational institutions preparing men for the priesthood and those of Protestant seminaries. In Catholic institutions, emphasis is placed on two full years of philosophy, where the required curriculum includes courses in logic, metaphysics, philosophy of human nature, natural theology, and ethics. Some Protestant seminaries require no philosophical preparation of their candidates for the ministry but place an emphasis on scriptural study and the languages required for exegesis. The Catholic seminary curriculum draws heavily on Aristotle in metaphysics and Aristotle and the Stoics in ethics, with the consequence that to the contemporary mind natural law ethics has come to be associated with Catholicism although it antedates Christianity itself.

MODERN INTERPRETATIONS

OF RELIGION, I

Hume, Kant, Hegel, Kierkegaard

With John Locke, David Hume (1711–76) is one of the most influential philosophers of the eighteenth century. Outside of philosophical circles, Hume is best known for his six-volume *History of England*, which appeared between 1754 and 1776. Following his death, at least fifty editions of his *History of England* appeared before 1894. He is regarded as one of the best writers of scientific prose in the history of English letters.[1]

Although Hume was brought up as a Calvinist, at a fairly early age he discarded those teachings. His doctrine of causality led him to deny that there is any evidence for the existence of God, a denial that had repercussions when he began his study of religion. Religion for him was a purely external phenomenon which aroused little or no response within himself. In this sense he was an irreligious man. But he acknowledged the part played by religion in the life of humanity, and he was interested in its nature and power.[2]

---

1. Cf. John Herman Randall, Jr., *The Making of the Modern Mind* (Cambridge, MA: Houghton Mifflin Co., 1940), 300ff.

2. *The Natural History of Religion*, edited by Wayne Colver (Oxford: At the Claren-

His systematic study of religion led him to the conclusion that religion was far from beneficial. He came to believe that religion impairs morality primarily by encouraging people to act for motives other than love of virtue for its own sake. Religion, he thought, is characterized by fanaticism, bigotry, and intemperate zeal. Yet Hume made an effort to distinguish between true religion, on the one hand, and superstition and fanaticism, on the other. The idea of the greatness and majesty of the infinite God associated with true religion has encouraged attitudes of abasement and practices of asceticism and mortification. These ideas were foreign to the pagan mentality.[3]

Hume's empirical approach to religion led him to the conclusion that belief in the existence of God is a natural belief, a habit or instinct of our nature. Of belief in the existence of God, Hume in his *Natural History of Religion* says that "if not an original instinct,[it is] at least a general attendant of human nature."[4] And in the *Treatise of Human Nature*, after arguing that no rational justification can be given for our belief in the existence of an external world except that we believe it because of our human nature, he draws the analogy between belief in the existence of God and belief in the existence of the external world. Belief in the existence of God is simply a habit of the mind due to our nature; "nothing

---

don Press, 1976), and *Dialogues Concerning Natural Religion*, edited by J. V. Price. (1779).

3. The *Dialogues Concerning Natural Religion* were published (1779) in accord with his wishes after his death. The *Natural History of Religion* appeared in 1757. The *Natural History* was most likely written between 1749 and 1751. During this period Hume was also engaged in writing his *Dialogues*. It is impossible to determine which he began first. Both volumes were complete before he was forty, after which he wrote no more original works in philosophy. The remainder of his career was spent writing his *History of England* or in revising his previously published philosophical works.

4. David Hume, *Natural History of Religion*, edited by T. H. Grose (London: Longmans Green, 1912), 215.

more is requisite to give a foundation to all the articles of religion."[5] Hume also maintained that natural religious beliefs have been distorted by "the incessant hopes and fears which activate the human mind." And he goes on to explain that "the anxious concern for happiness, the dread of future misery, the terror of death, the thirst for revenge, the appetite for good and other necessities" all have combined to distort the natural belief in God.[6] The implication is that if we could eliminate the effects of the various accidents and causes, then we would have the foundations of true religion.

But if belief is a natural habit, then the question of the existence of God is reduced to a question of anthropology. Habits can be acquired and changed; they can be either good or bad, either healthy or pathological. A habit as such justifies the truth value of nothing. It makes no sense to ask whether a habit is true or false, only whether it is good or bad, healthy or not, and whether or not it should be changed. Thus Hume treats religion and morality in a way that asserts the independence of morality from religion. He refuses to base the importance of religion on any contribution it supposedly makes toward morality.

Hume justifies his study of religion as one that is relevant, in fact indispensable, to a study of human nature. To understand man it is necessary to understand man as worshiper. In the study of religion it is not only important to examine topics traditionally labeled as religious in import, but it is absolutely necessary to examine those wellsprings in human nature itself from which the religious attitude and its interpretations of our existence a rise.

5. David Hume, *Treatise of Human Nature,* edited by L. A. Selby Biggs (Oxford: Clarendon Press, 1958), 533.
6. David Hume, *The Natural History of Religion,* 216.

The beliefs, strivings, and practical actions of the religious man are complex phenomena, phenomena that can be understood only in the light of one's general theory about human perceptions, association, and passions. A philosophical treatment of religion must proceed in two phases, steps that Hume calls: resolutive analysis and compositive synthesis.

As a complex human phenomenon, religion must be taken apart analytically and resolved into its component factors. A first objective is to clear up an ambiguity, i.e., one cannot take the religious complexus to mean a "particular *body of teaching*" at one time and a *characteristic human outlook* at another. There is a cognitive aspect of religion expressible eventually in a complex system of propositions, but this aspect is an outgrowth of some basic human attitudes. This human basis retains a controlling power over all doctrinal expressions of religion.

Analysis applies to the body of religious teachings chiefly by way of tracing them back to their sources in sustaining a human attitude. It then deals with the complex religious attitude itself by reducing it to certain component passional and cognitive principles. Hume identifies the elementary roots of religious belief in the passional drives of fear and hope, coupled with a lively concern to know the causes of events affecting our human welfare. Clearly religion posits a relational bond between man and God. What is one to do with the God-pole of the religious relationship since it is not subject to empirical investigation? Given Hume's general philosophy, God is removed, in principle, from investigation. Is the philosophical examination of religion thus hopelessly frustrated? Not at all.

The religious attitude involves a belief about some matters which fall within the realm of experience and some matters which do not. Hume can handle the matters which do not fall within experience in the same way he handles the problem of the external world. Within the methodological limits of his philosophy of human nature, he can specify the grounds in perception which lead men to believe in a powerful, minded being, existing independently of ourselves.

Hume is convinced that there is no other area of human experience where the play of the passions so strongly influences our beliefs. With respect to religious belief, there are no ready-made criteria for judging, such as are available in other disciplines. In ethics, you can check an argument against common human sentiment; in politics, if reason collides with matters of fact, you can check the facts, but no church can provide a universally accepted account of the nature of religion. Hume is convinced that he must rely on his personal experience. His inductive sources are limited to his own religious upbringing in Scotland, to his observation of religious conditions in Britain and France, to his study of the classical Roman accounts of religions, to the accounts of religion found in Bayle, and to his acquaintance with the tales of explorers and missionaries. While twentieth-century studies in comparative religion would have given Hume control over a greater range of materials, these may not have altered his analysis given his basic philosophical approach.

In evaluating religious phenomena Hume distinguishes between a preanalytic and a postanalytic form of obscurity and uncertainty and concludes that even after a careful analysis, there remains some postanalytic obscurity. His hope, he declares, is the modest one of merely establishing some points of orientation for understanding and evaluating man's religious commitments. Three areas are identified for investigation: first, the speculative justification of religion; second, the moral dimension of religion; and third, the relation between the natural knowledge provided by philosophy and faith in a divine revelation.

Two important subjects command his attention and are the focus of two major treatises: religion's foundation in reason and its origins in human nature. The *Natural History* is devoted mainly to religion's origin in human nature, the *Dialogues* to its foundations in reason. "Human nature," it should be noted, refers to the passional side of man. For Hume, religion is a response to a situation, but is that response instinctual or derivative? If it is a primary impulse, such as "self-love," comparable to "gravity," then it is analytically irreducible. It could figure in the explanation of other phenomena, but it could not itself be subjected to any penetrating genetic analysis. Upon reflection, Hume comes to the conclusion that religion is a composite, a derivative aspect of our passional life.

If religion were a primary impulse and analytically irreducible, nothing could be done about it. It would be an irreformable tendency of man without a history and without the possibility of being reformed. Thus Hume says, "The first religious principles must be secondary; such as may easily be perverted by various accidents and causes, and whose operation too, in some cases, may by an extraordinary concurrence of circumstances be altogether prevented."[7] Hume concludes that religion springs from passional tendencies which themselves are basic, permanent, and pervasive among men. Hence religion can be said to be natural to man. But this carries with it no guarantee about its human worth or the soundness of any religious conviction. The human heart is notorious for yielding both good fruit and bad.

In primitive man, religion is the child of fear and hope, stemming basically from fear, that is, from concern about the uncertainty and fragility of human existence. This fear is not stark terror, but has a certain imaginative and meditative dimension fostering

7. *The Natural History of Religion*, Section VII.

an enduring condition of human life. This fear involves a conception of natural events as being the manifestation of power exerted by unseen purposive agents. That there is an invisible intelligent power in the world is a belief common to all religions. From this belief follows another, namely, that man can relate himself to a presence which is invisible, mindful, and powerful. Hume makes much of a distinction between "popular religious belief" and "speculative theology." The popular religious attitude cannot rest originally upon a speculative theism. The dependence is the other way about. Our propensity to believe in a religious way is aroused by passions in the plural and is directed toward the many sorts of events and forces which powerfully affect our existence. Hence the primary religious outlook is polytheistic. Monotheism occurs later, as a refinement. In forming our fundamental religious response intelligence is operative, but it is not primary. Men are never led to religion by philosophical arguments, such as an argument to a first cause or from design in nature.

Although man comes to religion under the pressure of deep-seated fear and hope, sheer recognition of power in the world is not enough to constitute the religious attitude. A threefold response must occur. Men must relate themselves to it as agents, through some practical striving, and not merely as theoretical observers. This relationship must be suffused with a personal quality—the superior power has to be given a personal form. And finally, the development of the religious attitude requires men to feel deeply the tension between affirming a superior power beyond nature and seeking to relate oneself practically to it. Religious striving must be practical and personally ordered, but it must contain a definite strain of transcendence. Monotheism provides a superior account insofar as it focuses upon a concerned powerful reality which is immanent in the world but not as a component of na-

ture—personal and one, somehow transcending the limited con-
figuration of sensible things.

True to his antimetaphysical epistemology Hume rejects all argument for the existence of God, focusing his criticism on two
popular arguments: the *a priori* argument of Anselm and the argument from design. Not surprisingly, Hume rejects both.

Addressing the connection between religion and morality,
Hume thinks a purely secular morality is possible. He is convinced
that the separation of religion and morality can be achieved without injury to man's nature and to the order of values. There is no
connection between the design argument and morality. Religion
and morality are distinct and even disparate in their respective
bases and ultimate references, and in their motivations and consequences for human existence. Morality cannot afford to wait upon
the efforts of natural theology. Man must have some commonly
available principles and grounds for moral judgment.

In spite of his critical approach, Hume's interest was not nihilis-
tic. Religious belief, he holds, has an intrinsic structure which re-
sists reduction to natural theology, design speculation, and moral
principles. He acknowledges the distinctive nature of religious assent. It is clear that religious belief does not depend on demonstration. But how designate religious belief as a cognitive act? First, it
can be classified along with other complex ideas involving an
imaginative synthesis of many strains of meaning. Complex ideas
can be dissolved into their components. But we are dealing with a
complex idea which is also a belief. What is crucial for the religious
mind is its way of entertaining and interpreting impressions. The
mind does not meet the situation passively—the encounter is an
active one. Man comes to grips with the world through the mediation of his concrete intelligence that works along with hopes and
fears. Religious belief provides an integration of worldly experi-

ence with aspirations for happiness. No natural propensity is infallibly reliable and consequently should be subjected to philosophical criticism. Since religion is a natural propensity to seek divine aid in order to cope with the world, as such it has to be subjected to a radical and persistent skeptical inspection. Interestingly Hume finds that even after such skeptical treatment, belief is God remains and is not diminished to the extent one might expect.

Contrary to Paul Henri Dietrich Holbach (1723–89), who expected that upon criticism, religious belief would shrivel up and disappear, Hume maintained that one's assent to God's reality may be deprived of many customary supports in argument without being annihilated or reduced to the status of a stubborn social custom. Its persistence may be taken as a sign of the totally noncognitive basis of religious belief. But that is not all that Hume is saying. Even the sophisticated inquire about the orderly aspects of the natural world, believing that they represent the powerful presence of a transcendent mind. The sophisticated believer will not claim that he has demonstrative scientific knowledge of God. But he will recognize some grounds within his own questioning nature, and within the visible world for believing.

A man formed by Hume's philosophy of nature cannot remain either an untroubled dogmatist or an untroubled skeptic. He is compelled to give a cautious, highly qualified assent to the religious reference of human life. Put succinctly, belief is generated by man's passionate search for happiness and his anxious scrutiny of the aspects of design in nature. A philosophical critique of religion frees one from both popular belief and skepticism. The mind which reflects upon the nature of religious belief will consequently emerge with a transformed view of theism and religion.

The philosopher cannot remain satisfied with the popular forms of religion. He tries to determine that conception of religion which will survive the most severe skeptical questioning and furthermore be compatible with a nonreligious morality. He is thus brought to distinguish several forms of popular theism, namely, religious monotheism, its derivative theology, and an uncritical philosophical theism. The latter is seen as a form of abstract apology for monotheistic religion. These three are further distinguished from critical philosophical theism, "genuine theism" or the probable speculative assent to God—which gives rise to "true religion."

Hume's critical philosophical theism is monotheistic. It takes account of the intellectual developments of mankind, particularly the work of philosophers who have achieved a unified view of nature and incorporates the work of modern scientists who view nature in terms of mechanical and organic models. In the wake of these interpretations, it is reasonable to believe that there is one supreme mind shaping the forces of nature. This likelihood, however, is tempered but not destroyed by considering the contrary evidences of counter-purpose, viz., evil and the randomness also apparent in the world. Hume's theism is speculative without moral connotations.

In sum, religion as endorsed by Hume is confined to the act of giving a probable speculative assent to a cosmic mind. Hume draws no practical consequences. To know God is to worship Him. All other worship is indeed absurd, superstitious, and even impious. Centuries later, a prominent American philosophy will speak of "our obligation to know God" in the sense specified by Hume and mean by it something other than the biblical mandate of Western Christendom. Hume is aware that a philosophically reformed religion is viable only for a few reflective minds. Even so, philosophical assent should be given only when the inquiring mind is actually focused on the divine. Religion is definitely not a habitual principle of thought and action.

In spite of analysis, religious belief remains a mystery. Hume realizes that his account will not satisfy the ordinary believer. He acknowledges that the propensity toward religious belief arises from some deep-seated passions which are ordered toward action and that no amount of philosophical criticism will eradicate it.

Immanuel Kant (1724–1804), following the lead of David Hume, similarly produced a comprehensive philosophy of religion, defending the reasonableness of belief in spite of reason's inability to demonstrate the existence of God. His theory of religion is part of his philosophical system and is governed by his conception of the nature, aim, and method of philosophy. For Kant, the task of philosophy is largely therapeutic. Its obligation is to criticize and reform. In his three famous *Critiques* he addresses three questions: In the *Critique of Pure Reason,* the question "What can I know?"; in the *Critique of Practical Reason,* "What ought I to do?"; and in the *Critique of Judgment,* "What may I hope?"[8]

Kant's theory of religion arises as he attempts to answer the third question. The theme of hope is central to his critical work. Kant read Hume's *Dialogues* in 1780, and convinced by Hume that we cannot demonstrate the existence of God, Kant opens the way to a practical foundation for belief in the existence of God. Although he was to abandon the religion of his pietist upbringing, Kant never withdrew his assent to a personal theism. In agreement

8. The definitive edition of Kant's *opera omnia* is the Prussian Academy edition, *Gesammelte Schriften,* 24 vols. (Berlin: Walter de Gruyter, 1902–66). An appreciative guide to his work and his place in the history of philosophy is provided by Frederick Copelston, S. J., in *A History of Philosophy,* Vol. VI, *Wolf to Kant* (Westminster, MD: The Newman Press, 1960). This chapter relies heavily on its interpretation of Kant on Copelston and on James Collins, *The Emergence of Philosophy of Religion* (New Haven, CT: Yale University Press, 1967). The Cambridge University Press editions of specific works by Kant which deal with religion are noted below.

with Jean Jacques Rousseau he sought a foundation for religious belief in the "moral personality."

Situated in the context of his three critiques the principal source of his philosophy of religion is found in *Religion within the Limits of Reason Alone*. That publication was followed by *The End of All Things*, a work which stresses the religious importance of love and hope, and *The Metaphysics of Morals*, which rejects the classical notion that religion is a set of duties owed in justice to God. A work published just a year later entitled *The Strife of Faculties* explores the educational implications of his thought.[9] In this work he defends the right of philosophy to make its own examination of the meaning of religion and even of revelation against encroachment from either the state or the theologians.

Kant's philosophy of religion has to be seen against the backdrop of the seventeenth-century pietist movement, a religious revival which originated in Germany as a reaction to the Lutheran theology of his day. The pietists regarded the Christian faith not as a set of doctrinal propositions to which the believer must subscribe but as a living relationship with God. They stressed the power of God to transform the believer's life through a conversion or a rebirth experience. Like orthodox Lutheranism, pietism exalted the authority of Scripture above that of natural reason. It was hostile to the Hellenization of Christianity, including the systematic study of Sacred Scripture, insisting that the Bible be read for inspiration and moral edification. Pietists, as their name might suggest, favored the cultivation of piety and morality rather than

---

9. *Religion within the Limits of Reason Alone, The End of All Things, The Strife of Faculties, Lectures on the Philosophical Doctrine of Religion* (1817), and other texts have been collected in a single volume, *Religion and Rational Theology,* translated and edited by Allen W. Wood and George Di Giovanni (Cambridge: Cambridge University Press, 1996), providing ready access to Kant's philosophy of religion.

theoretical enquiry. Kant's attitude toward his pietist background was ambivalent. He rejected pietism's anti-intellectualism, but much of his conception of morality and religion, as we shall see, may be regarded as a rationally purified version of pietism. A believing philosopher, Kant concludes, can engage in radical criticism of speculative demonstration without undermining his religious convictions. One must believe, he maintains, even if one can't demonstrate. If one can't say "*It is* morally certain that there is a God," one can say, "*I am* morally certain there is a God." Implicit is a distinction between revealed religion and the natural religion of reason. Although Kant admits of no argument for the existence of God, his critical philosophy after making a negative assessment of the speculative proofs for failing to reckon with the limits of reason and human experience attempts to salvage what it can.

The object of Kant's criticism is speculative proof in the manner of the Scholastics, not speculative theology. He does not abandon the entire body of speculative thought about God but remains convinced that even if the arguments did succeed, they would lead to a view of God inconsistent with theistic realism. God would necessarily be conceived after the manner of a phenomenological object or a lawgiver, which conception is at variance with traditional religious belief.

While arguments for the existence of God can never have a demonstrative force, they can nevertheless serve an incitive role. Such arguments function to keep our minds alive to the importance of existential questions about God. We never approach the question of God's existence in a purely detached manner. All questions about God have a practical effect. Hence, all the components in our speculative idea of God can be integrated, in principle, with the moral meaning of God.

Examining the genesis of religious belief, Kant concludes that several cognitive faculties are brought into play in the act of belief. The cognitive basis of assent follows either the ways of imagination, i.e., concrete imagining or intuitive vision, contrasted with the ways of reason, i.e., speculative proof or moral belief. Concrete imagining leads to idolatrous superstition; intuitive vision to enthusiastic fanaticism. Speculative proof leads to metaphysical theologism; moral belief to moral theism.

Kant sees an historical progression from imagination to reason. Historically considered even before men engage in formal theological speculations, their practical moral impulse enables them to make a preliminary passage from polytheism to moral monotheism. In its initial condition, moral theism is quite vulnerable and weak. In the past men have tried to shore it up by placing it on a speculative footing, treating religion as though it were a practical consequence drawn from metaphysical reasoning. Yet metaphysical theism has never been able to sustain its own claims; thus its long-range influence has been more unsettling rather than stabilizing.

As a result of theological controversies, religious believers tend in self-defense to subordinate the way of reason to that of imagination. The descent from speculative proof to visionary enthusiasm in religious matters is swift and often goes undetected. When people do recognize this fluctuation between pretended speculative proof and pretended spiritual vision, their adherence to God is fundamentally shaken. Skepticism in religious questions is a protected response. To overcome visionary enthusiasms, one cannot appeal to still further speculative demonstrations. Kant recommends instead that the distinctive resources of moral belief be freed from theologism and integrated, instead, with a critique of knowledge and a reflective understanding of human history and cultural growth. In this context, Kant makes a distinction between the "precritical" and "the modern critico-historical" condition of moral theism. A critico-historical approach shows that the demand to gain speculative demonstrations about God is unwarranted and oversteps the limits of human reason. Once this demand has been systematically removed, the human mind is relieved of the pressure to overcompensate by means of an intuitive vision of spiritual reality.

To believe is to accept as certain and true, and hence to assent to, those realities which are implicated in our moral freedom and obligation, but which are not available to intuition or demonstration. The act of believing is not a step along the path of speculative knowledge. Belief is a cognitive way of its own. It requires a distinctive disposition of the mind while the mind operates under a distinctive maxim of reason. A modern person, alive to the challenges of skepticism and naturalism in religious matters, must adopt a distinctive orientation of mind in order to believe. This can only come after a deliberate process of reflection and gradual orientation.

Kant identifies four steps in reflective preparation. First we must make sure that the subject of the search does not fall within the scope of knowledge and opinion; second, that it contains no contradiction and survives the test for internal consistency; third, that it is coherent with what we do know. Only then can we make a comparison between the limits of human knowing and the drive to increase our cognitive act so that it may somehow include the divine reality lying beyond the range of objective knowledge as such.

Once we recognize this discrepancy between what we can know and what we seek to cognize in some other fashion, our reason necessarily generates the feeling of a cognitive need for relying on some act of faith. Although reason itself does not feel, it brings this feeling of a need before itself. In short, the cognitive mind orients itself toward belief, which then serves as the grounding principle of man's acceptance of God. Thus, belief may be said to rest upon a subjective principle of certainty, following up a reflective awareness of a need for faith on the part of the active personal subject. Religious believers may not always explicitly go through the four stages, yet there is always some minimal reflection present in moral belief. Kant insists that reflection yields an informal yet reasonable knowledge of God that can be developed into the attitude of belief (of course, within the atmosphere of modern criticism).

Belief is not to be equated with wishful thinking. Rational moral belief is genuine only when assent is determined by some necessary need. Rational belief stems from a judgment regarding the structure of man's free moral agency. The task of moral philosophy and its continuation in the theory of religion is to test the claim of specific candidates for moral belief.

Doctrinal beliefs by contrast are derivative. They do not enjoy the same direct founding. They merely serve as an instrumental character to moral belief. Theoretical doctrinal beliefs concerning God help to explicate the meaning of moral theism and to prepare for its intellectual analysis and defense. They are propoedutic, constituting the *organon* of our moral belief in God, but they cannot serve as its fundament. Speculative theology is thus subordinate to moral belief.

Kant addresses the question of whether we can affirm the objective reality of God in Whom we have moral faith? His reply comes in three parts: First, he denies that moral belief affirms anything to be real and objective in the same way in which the objects and *a priori* conditions of our physical knowledge are real and objective.

Second, he maintains that something has moral reality or objectivity insofar as it is a component of human freedom and moral law, or is necessarily related in some way with man's condition as a moral agent. In this manner, "freedom" itself is affirmed to be objectively real. As moral agents under the law, men are free. Since belief in God rests on an inference made from our moral situation and expresses an implication inherent in that situation as shared by all men, this belief also affirms a real and objective truth in the moral order. Third, even though we succeed in keeping God distinct from the objects and laws in nature, there is the danger of taking His objective reality to mean that belief in Him is an impersonal truth. To avoid this danger, we must make a distinction between the "content of belief" and the "act of believing." The former can be shared by all men, but each man must make his own personal act of faith. The act of believing is a free personal response. It is not like a conclusion reached as a result of demonstration. Assent is not determined solely by impersonal considerations. Belief springs into existence only when an individual makes a personal discovery of the involvement of God in his own moral situation. The key word for the moral theist is not *crede* but *credo*.

Kant repudiates the Humean split between popular and philosophical religion. Some knowledge of God is required in order that there be a religious referring of our duties. Theological knowledge assists the development of the life of virtue by encouraging us to view moral duties as if they were divine commands; it grounds the basic religious responses of hope, fear, and love of God; and it is important for engaging in ecclesial services of the visible church.

Morality necessarily leads to religion. There is a continuity between respect for the moral law and reverence for God. Our direct response to God is made through the religious attitudes of reverence, love, and respectful fear. The act of reverence arises from the correlation in man between his law-giving moral reason and his view of God as the holy source of laws. Similarly, religious love is sustained by the dynamism coming from our desire for happiness and our moral notion of the good Lord. Our respectful fear arises from the interaction between conscience and the attribution of incorruptible justice to God. Moral reason as legislative leads to reverence; our inclination to happiness to love; and our conscience to fear. God is seen as a holy lawgiver, a benevolent provider of happiness, and a just judge.

Believers not only give a religious interpretation to moral duties but also engage themselves in specifically religious practices and institutions. This is to be regarded as laudable. Kant's aim is not to suppress the movement beyond the minimum, but he does wish to ensure some sort of philosophical control over further elaborations.

Kant is aware of the actual pluralism of religions. He read the best scholarly studies in comparative religion made during the seventeenth and eighteenth centuries. In addition he was familiar with the *Rig Veda,* the *Zendavesta,* and the *Koran,* but he concentrated on Christianity.

For Kant, the view of man and God provided by the Bible is readily susceptible to a moral and religious interpretation, because there is a certain consistent wholeness about the Bible.

On the other hand, some of Kant's contemporaries do not find it so easy to accommodate biblical religion. Holbach, for example, denies the reality of a divine being, and thereby eliminates the possibility of revelation. Kant explicitly rejects Holbach as well as Voltaire's philosophical theism, which admits a personal God and even a kind of revelation from Him but identifies that revelation with whatever can be determined by philosophical reason. Kant asserts that Voltaire arbitrarily restricts the entire meaning of religion to its philosophically elaborated content and consequently dispenses completely with the historical and institutional aspects of revealed religion—things Kant is not willing to ignore. The invisible, Kant maintains, needs to be represented through the visible. Revelational religion performs this incarnation and sacramental function, with the result that we can permeate our imagery, our practical decisions, and our historical striving with religious significance. Against this backdrop we can now understand why philosophy of religion is not concerned exclusively with pure moral religion or consists exclusively in an exegesis of revelational religion. Of necessity religion must realize itself in a social manner, even in visible ecclesiastical institutions. Philosophy must analyze the manifestations of the concrete religious spirit and determine their general human significance. In doing so, it can discuss the visible organization, statutes, rites, scriptural statements, traditions of learning, and regional establishments as supported by political ordinances and civil power.

The transition from the pure idea of religion to the human modes of referring conduct to God is, in fact, a transition to the realm of the morally good and evil acts of men in the plural and in the social group. Together, men corrupt each other, and together they work out the social conditions for achieving a virtuous and religiously ordered life.

A religion of pure moral belief is not enough. Religion must develop social forms which take account of the practical mediation of the human community in our movements toward God or away from Him. Human religion cannot consist solely of the mystical flight of "the alone to the alone." Of necessity such a relationship always requires some support from and some implications for the wider human community. Man is responsible not only for regulating his own conduct by the principle of morality but also for doing whatever he can toward aiding other men in accepting a similar ground for action. He must share his moral maxim with others. He must unite with others in socially effective ways that encourage their personal adherence to morality, ways that lessen their vulnerability to social forces inimical to the moral disposition. This is accomplished through the personal dispositions of love and community dedication.

Kant defines love as "the free reception of the will of another person into one's own maxims."[10] It opens us out responsibly to the interior struggle of other men to achieve a virtuous life. Love is a forceful reminder of moral interdependence. The highest good is social. The basic question, "What may I hope for?" may be reframed, "What may we hope for together?" God is seen as the Lord of the ethical commonwealth, as the common hope for men who are striving together to realize a social good which may not lie entirely within human power.

God is a powerful moral unifier not only of *nature* and *man* but also of *man* and *man*. What unites the moral believers in God is their joint practical conviction that the divine will is good and holy. To regard our ethical duties as divine commands that are in accord with the religious reference of our social life strengthens, rather than jeopardizes, the primacy of the moral principle and the integrity of personality within the ethical community united under God. A commonwealth thus united under divine laws constitutes the City of God or the invisible church. Properly considered, it is a union of hearts and wills, a family relationship, a people of God.

In the ideal case, if men were pure rational agents, this invisible union might suffice. But men being composite, experience-bound agents, it does not. The passage from the invisible to the visible

---

10. *The End of All Things* in *On History*, edited by L. W. Beck, Bobbs-Merrill (1963), 82.

church responds to a need of our actually constituted human reality.

Statutory religion, as it was known in the Europe of his time, says Kant, infringes on our intellectual and moral freedom. It transforms the free assent of faith into a servile, coerced, and mercenary act. Our relationships to God become either a purely public profession or a favor-currying bond. In such an atmosphere, one's moral disposition is reduced to third place, well behind a careful observance of statutes and a careful participation in the visible rites of worship. Religious sociality suffers in being narrowed down to the visible church. When practical religious life gravitates entirely around publicly sanctioned religion, believers tend to forget their inner commitment and their familial relationship with God and each other. Kant wishes to affirm the primacy of the invisible union of believers with God, yet he recognizes that the concrete realization of the religious community depends on the visible church.

If the visible commonwealth is genuinely interested in the welfare of religion, it will observe a self-limitation in its support of a religious establishment and in its demand that citizens accept a statutory faith. There is a mean between the extremes of imposing the established religion upon everyone and treating the visible church as an unmitigated obstacle to the religious spirit. The moral center of religion cannot be coerced by law. The church which chooses establishment above religious freedom is choosing to make itself something other than authentic religion.

Kant strongly defends academic freedom in religious matters. Of necessity there will be a permanent conflict among the scriptural exegete, the theologian of revelation, and the moral philosopher interested in revealed religion. It is in the interest of both religion and philosophy to encourage this academic life. The political commonwealth should respect the freedom of religious discussion within the university and the context of learning. Each has "authority" within its own realm.

In clarifying the sense in which the spiritual union of wills constitutes the one, true church, Kant discusses the marks of the church. Traditionally these marks were specified as "one," "holy," "catholic," and "apostolic." Within Kant's philosophical approach, the marks of the true church are those traits which constitute the attitude of pure moral religion, and hence which indicate its presence in any given church. For Kant they are unity, holiness, freedom, and unchangeable intention.

The true church is one because it consists of those common truths about the religious relating of man to God which can in principle be apprehended by all men who have the use of practical reason. It is holy insofar as it rests on the moral ordering of motives, which ought to ensure that our wills are referred first of all to morality itself and then to the holy, good, and powerful God. Its freedom specifies that the relationship of any religious believers is familial, which steers clear of organizational imposition on the one hand and private illumination on the other. Its unchangeable intention means that the people of God possess the undeviating aim to join minds and hearts together for the practical purpose of becoming better men.

Christianity has a Sacred Scripture and must eventually organize a tradition of commentary on the Scripture through the resources of philology, history, and philosophy. Inevitably it must use learning in order to fathom and to communicate its message as revealed religion and as support of a visible church. On the side of the believers, there must be a learned public devoted to the logical study of the Christian gospel and to its implementation in a set of statues to be obeyed by the majority of men who cannot follow the learned discussions. The morals of unity are obscured by both the learned discussion and the statues. A religion mediated by learning is not universally communicable to all men. One mediated by particular statues is likewise restricted. Thus the complex structure of historical Christianity both favors and hinders the actualization of religious unity among men.

Kant sometimes distinguishes between two functions of theological learning: to clarify the meaning of religion and to communicate the religious knowledge from one generation to another. Learning serves to clarify the religious message without becoming the necessary means of communicating it. In actual religious life, the message is brought to men through preaching, dialogue, and catechesis. These are the living means for communicating the word of God which is not conveyed primarily through research and statutory laws.

Religion must somehow be historical. Our religious disposition is freely originated, but it must endure and bear fruits within the temporal world. The religious orientation of one's life does not occur in an instant. Similarly with the visible church: its history is the history of a struggle to fulfill its mission as the human instrument in the realization of moral fulfillment.

As distinct from various church histories, the religious history of humanity is the story of the developing teleological relations between the visible church and the invisible church or family of God. There is a steady common orientation of all visible forms of religion toward the pure moral meaning of religion, a striving to realize the human nucleus of religion under the social and historical conditions of our race. The chronicling of this is the moral history of religion.

The philosopher can interest himself in theological teachings about death, judgment, heaven, and hell, as materials that reveal of the structure of human nature. From these he can develop a philo-

sophical eschatology. Philosophy seeks to join a theoretical knowledge of the natural world with a practical understanding of man's
moral life. The aim of philosophy is wisdom, just as the aim of
Christianity is holiness. Philosophy doesn't succeed in bringing the
two together. Wisdom and holiness are one in God, but in man
they remain distinct practical goals to be sought. The philosopher
may study religion, but when his study is complete, he must still
respect the autonomous religious wisdom of the holy man of God.

While rejecting Holbach and Voltaire, Kant is not willing to
identify with those who make the Bible the primary norm of reasonableness. The approach of the latter, no less than that of Holbach and Voltaire, constitutes a threat against the humane approach which Kant is attempting to develop. If we must first know
that an action is a divine command before we can be sure about its
religious and moral worth, we cut off the native roots of moral and
religious conviction. Experience would cease to be the foundation-
al act. In that case, any harmony between biblical religion and philosophical reflection is rendered insignificant. Philosophy should
move parallel to biblical theology. Theologians should not panic
and attempt to place revelational religion entirely beyond the scope
of rational reflection.

Kant was consistent in his opposition to irrationalism in religion. The mature person, called upon to make a religious response, must be able to discern a need in the human condition for
divine aid in the form of historical revelation. He must be able to
compare the message provided by Sacred Scripture with his inner
moral ideal of God. Hence, revelation must present itself as a realization of man's religious reflections and moral aspirations. A revelation proposed solely by appeal to divine power and authority or
to some already constituted set of civil and ecclesiastical ordinances would not manifest to us the morally good and just God. It
would leave out love. Kant called his own position a "pure" or

"nonreductive rationalism." Thus, Kant says that distinction between natural and revealed religion is misleading. Whenever our religious assent and practice are involved, both faith and reason are present in some sense. An act of belief is essential to the assent given in the pure moral form of religion; on the other hand, practical reason is fully engaged in the assent given to Christian revelation in its moral significance. Christian revelation speaks a message to man in his practical reason. It seeks to aid mankind in realizing its common moral good in the social order.

Kant distinguishes among statutory, supernatural, and instrumental religion, which are meanings not usually distinguished. *Statutory* or ecclesiastical faith is determined by the creed and practice of a church and reinforced by civil ordinances. *Supernatural* faith is the doctrinal truths and practices which are supernatural in their origin. *Instrumental* religion is the vehicle or concrete instrument for the realization of moral theism under human conditions.

The philosophy of religion, says Kant, treats revelation from the instrumental standpoint only. There is bound to be a difference between religion treated from the instrumental perspective of philosophy and the supernatural perspective of the theology of revelation. The three cannot be perfectly synthesized unless one were to deny the perspective of one or the other, something Kant is not willing to do. Revelational religion may contain something which no philosophy can grasp within the limits of its own insight. So, philosophy of religion developed within the human condition must recognize its limits. It must refrain from denying the supernatural. It may even recognize the need for God's supernatural initiative at an historical moment in which mankind is introduced to the insights provided in revelational religion, although thereafter a philosophical analysis and grounding of them can be made.

In the practical order, and especially in confrontation with evil, the religious man may become aware of the need for supernatural help. This "something more" may be required for the integrity and perfection of human action. The supernatural aspect of revelation, of course, is entirely beyond the range of philosophical investigation. It remains totally unassimilable to practical reason and underivable from the moral imperative. It is a mystery which cannot be denied but also one which cannot be communicated to us, neither by God in the form of a speculative truth nor through philosophical reasoning. The supernatural and instrumental or philosophical conceptions of revelation cannot be synthesized.

As far as concerns the philosophy of religion, revelation can only be regarded as a process of concretization and humanization. The process is required if the meanings involved in the pure moral conception of religion are not to remain mere empty ideals without objective practical content. They must be brought down to human soil. The pure moral view of religion has to be adapted to sensible events and the flow of history.

The revelational mode of religion may be called "applied religion," an instrument for giving practical human support to our minimal religious belief. The Bible, for example, uses concrete imagery and symbols and is concerned with the temporal and historical aspect of God's presence in history. Scripture, tradition, and the visible church contribute to the practical union of men. The religious imagery furnished by revelation, together with history and the ecclesial community, make our moral theism relevant to the sphere of human action and thus achieve objective practical value for religious meanings, and in doing so meet a deep-seated human need.

From this brief presentation, it is evident that Kant offers a well-developed and lofty conception of religion. Although he denies that there is demonstrative evidence for the existence of God, he nevertheless insists on the reasonableness of belief in God. While he does not share the rational preamble of Aquinas, he sets forth a sequence of steps implicitly requisite for the act of faith. In emphasizing the relation between morality and faith, he is clearly aware of the role that religion plays in society. Religion, far from being a private affair, requires an institutional structure, a "visible church," (although establishment itself is not desirable). He appreciates the moral and tutorial role of the Bible but nevertheless reserves for reason the function of judgment. The sage of Königsburg is equally removed from the secularity and anticlerical outlook of the French Enlightenment and from the hierarchical, episcopal, and Roman Church. As the architect of a comprehensive philosophy of religion, Kant is clearly unsurpassed for his period, and his work remains a vital source for the philosophical study of religion.

Georg Wilhelm Hegel (1770–1831) began to lecture on religion in 1821 and in the next decade produced what we know as his *Lectures on the Philosophy of Religion*.[11] Hegel's study of religion is not unlike that employed in this volume. After exploring the concept of religion—"Religion is a consciousness of the absolute universal object"[12]—he first examines its concrete manifestations in magic and then its manifestations in Daoism, Buddhism, and Hinduism, as well as its expressions in Egypt, Persia, Greece, Israel, and Rome.[13]

To adequately treat Hegel's monumental work in the philoso-

---

11. G. W. Hegel, *Lectures on the Philosophy of Religion*, 2 vols. edited by Peter C. Hodgson, translated by R. F. Brown, P. C. Hodgson and J. M. Stewart (Berkeley: University of California Press, 1984–87).

12. Hegel, *Lectures, 1824, Ibid.*, Vol. I, 317.

13. Hegel, *Lectures, 1827, Ibid.*, Vol. II, 535–696.

phy of religion would require a volume in itself. Our purpose is served with a brief summary indicating his place in the ongoing nineteenth century debate concerning the nature of religion. At the beginning of the nineteenth-century, the philosophy of religion was a novel topic, not part of the ordinary agenda of the philosopher. Indebted to Kant, Hegel nevertheless takes issue with him on a number of key issues, specifically on what we can know of God. "For the doctrine that we can know nothing of God, that we cannot cognitively apprehend him," writes Hegel, "has become in our time a universally acknowledged truth, a settled thing, a kind of prejudice."[14] Challenging this prejudice, Hegel writes, "I declare such a point of view . . . to be directly opposed to the whole nature of the Christian religion, according to which we should *know* God *cognitively;* God's nature and essence, and should esteem this cognition above all else." [italics Hegel's][15] Hegel affirms that philosophy itself has as its object the true, and the true in its highest shape, as absolute Spirit, as God. "To know this true not only in its simple form as God, but to know the rational in God's works—as produced by God and endowed with reason—that is philosophy."[16] Stated in a cursory way, Hegel recognized that religion is our relation to God. "This relation is found in thinking."[17]

Hegel criticizes Kant on the supposed moral basis of religion. The religious attitude, Hegel maintains, cannot be based on hope; it can only be based on love. Religion is the fulfillment of love, not an extension of moral duty. Jesus raises mankind above the spirit of Kantian morality by changing the passage from "shalt" to "is," from an imposed command to the free acceptance of reality as the principle of moral action and religious loyalty. Religious love is an

---

14. G. W. Hegel, *Lectures, Ibid.,* Vol. I, 86.   15. Ibid., 88.
16. Ibid., 446.   17. Ibid., 448.

inclination so to act as the laws may command. Hegel thus reverses the relationship between morality and religion. Religion, Hegel maintains, is a spur to philosophy. Religious faith stirs up the subjective energies in the human existent. It impels him on a lifelong quest for the intellectual grounds of his religious interpretations of life and for the practical means of bringing his ideal to realization. Gradually, it dawns on him that the relationship between philosophy and religion is not precisely an instrumental one but rather one of organic maturation. The theoretical and practical truths he once held on faith can eventually be held through a philosophically motivated judgment. The act of faith and that of philosophical knowing stand related as the implicit and explicit stages of a single growth in awareness. Religion is philosophy grasped in the mode of groping presentiment, whereas philosophy is religion brought to its internal fulfillment and conscious articulation. It is the same person who says the creed as a young man and as an old man. Wisdom comes to him when he recognizes that the aim of his eager religious search for understanding is fully realized in the methods and judgments constituting his philosophical knowledge. He sees that philosophy is religion's deeper and truer self, the unfolded truth concerning the certainties of religious faith and practice.

To determine the precise ordering between religion and philosophy is a task for the philosophy of religion. The philosophical examination of religion must respect the general solidarity of religion with other components in human culture and examine religion within its own cultural situation. Religion, Hegel is convinced, is bound up with the whole network of cultural forms in which man's nature actually displays itself and develops. Hence, primary attention must be given to the broad social matrix of religion. The philosopher must show how this particular religious outlook is both formed within and adapted to a specific cultural situation.

One necessarily begins with the modern world, a world which embodies the religious heritage of Greece and the ancient world religions, especially Christianity in its biblical presentation. But modernity places a unique stamp upon these human materials by reinterpreting them in the light of decisive steps taken in the Reformation, the Enlightenment, and the French Revolution. When religious modernity is understood in this ample sense, there is nothing parochial about requiring the philosophical approach to religion to begin with an assessment of the here-and-now actuality of religious life before offering its strongest criticisms of that actuality.

Any appraisal of the modern condition of religion has to take notice of the fateful shift in the scales of knowledge and interest. The more our knowledge of and control over finite things has increased, the more our claims to possess knowledge of God have weakened. Our interest in the practical has led us away from religious values. "There was a time when one had the interest, the drive, to know about God, to fathom His nature, when the spirit had found no rest except in this occupation. . . . Our time has renounced this need and its toils."[18]

This shift in interest is mirrored in the attempt of Schleiermacher to push dogma into the background and to center the philosophy of religion on our attitude and feeling rather than upon the being of God as its specifying goal. Hegel does not bemoan this shift. He is concerned with it in order to discern the presence and power of religion in the world. For him this is the starting point of the philosophy of religion.

Hegel rejects the view that there is only one natural religion

18. Ibid., 86.

with many contra-natural positive religions because such a view rests upon a questionable appeal to human nature as a nonhistorical, atemporal entity. The supposition underlying that view is that human nature is constituted by a few invariant concepts. The criterion for natural religion would then be the restriction of religious belief to the purity of this conceptual definition of human nature. Any variations and additions to this definition would serve to characterize a religion as "positive" and, ultimately, as opposed to "natural" religion.

Hegel posits instead that the naturalness of religion consists in its being an appropriate expression of a segment of man's needs and feelings, taken concretely within a particular temporal context and historical stage of development. Our historically qualified "human nature" of necessity leads us to recognize a Being beyond human agency Who transcends the temporal. We make the intuition that that Being's perfection is the animating spirit of human life, and devote time, feelings, and organizations directly to this intuition independently of other aims.

The religious exigency of human nature can only be satisfied in ways that are inescapably complex, plural, and historically developing. In this sense there can be, and indeed must be, many modes of natural religion. Hence, natural religion is not one unchanging, abstract core of concepts but lives in and through the entire historical pattern of man's many religious beliefs and practices. Religious life is a mixed affair, profoundly ambiguous; it is both natural and positive. Religious faith stirs up the subjective energies in the human existent. It impels him on a lifelong quest for the intellectual grounds of his religious interpretations of life.

Asserting the primacy of philosophy over religion, Hegel maintains that the meaning, validity, and truth of religion are to be adjudicated by philosophy. The religious sphere opens one to the spiritual, but it is penultimate, not ultimate. Religion relies on imagery and pictorial representation and is consequently inadequate. The religious insight sought in parables and through pictorial artifacts is to be filtered and reinterpreted by philosophy where ambiguity can be recognized and settled with certainty. Hegel was convinced that the religious belief of any age was one of its shaping principles that determined its cultural outlook.

It is difficult to underestimate the influence of Kant on nineteenth- and twentieth-century thought in Europe and the Americas. On the subject of belief, his influence is seen dramatically in the work of Søren Kierkegaard (1811–55) who became popular with American audiences in the mid-decades of the twentieth-century although he published in the nineteenth. Kant also exercised considerable influence on the American philosophers Josiah Royce, Arthur Lovejoy, and William James, all widely read philosophers who developed Kantian themes at length, but it is Kierkegaard who commands our present attention because he takes one element of Kant to an extreme.

Kierkegaard is only one of many nineteenth-century philosophers who, following the lead of Kant and Hegel, took it to be one of their principal tasks to criticize Christianity on presumably philosophical grounds. Karl Löwith notes that, "Philosophical criticism of the Christian religion began in the nineteenth century with Hegel and reached its climax with Nietzsche. It is a Protestant movement, and therefore specifically German; this holds true of both the criticism and the religion at which it was directed. Our critical philosophers were all educated Protestants, and their criticism of Christianity presupposes its Protestant manifestation."[19]

In the long line of theologians stretching from Luther himself to Brunner, Barth, and Bultmann, Kierkegaard holds a unique

19. Karl Löwith, *From Hegel to Nietzsche: The Revolution in 19th Century Thought* (New York: Columbia University Press, 1991), 327–28.

place. He was the first to state, in more or less modern form, the case against rationalism.[20] Luther had stated it before him, but the rationalism Luther opposed was the comparatively modest rationalism of the Schoolman and Erasmus. What Kierkegaard had to contend with was the rationalism of Hegel. Drawing upon Kant in his attack on Hegel, he goes one step further, robbing religion, specifically Christianity, of any "objective" content. Faith is not a matter of belief that can be set forth in propositional form, nor is religion a rational affair.

Making a distinction between the world of universals (scientific generalizations) and the subjective world (inwardness), Kierkegaard will say that whereas philosophy teaches us to become objective, Christianity teaches us to become subjective, to face our existence and cease avoiding it by scientific generalizations. This is not easy. We are constantly tempted to fit ourselves into received categories, to speak of ourselves in heroic terms borrowed from patterns we have seen elsewhere.

Evidence for God's existence is an "objective question," but we find no conclusive evidence for His existence. Whether we can demonstrate the existence of God or not makes no difference from the standpoint of faith. Far more important is what happens to the individual when he is called upon to believe that which cannot be objectively known. With respect to objective matters, there will always be doubt. What is important is what happens to the individual in the face of doubt. The believer is not turned away by objective uncertainty but instead passionately affirms. Kierkegaard calls this "subjective truth." Subjective truth is not truth in the usual sense; it is what is usually called "faith."

---

20. Søren Kierkegaard, *Either/Or.* 2 vols., Vol. I, translated by David F. Swenson, Lillian Swenson, and Marvin Swenson; Vol. II, translated by Howard A. Johnson (Princeton, NJ: Princeton University Press, 1944).

Faith is precisely the contradiction between the infinite passion of the individual's inwardness and objective uncertainty. If I am capable of grasping God objectively, I am not believing, but precisely because I cannot so grasp God, I must believe. If I wish to preserve myself in faith, I must constantly be intent on holding fast the objective uncertainty, so as to remain out upon the deep, over seventy thousand fathoms of water, still preserving my faith.[21]

Faith is thus defined as subjective conviction; objective uncertainty. The spiritual growth required to make the leap of faith is important to the individual as a human being, as a moral agent. The man who tries to believe by the use of reason rather than against reason is comic.

For Kierkegaard, the question Christianity tries to answer is, "What does the individual, the subject, count for?" In the ultrarationally interpreted world he counts for little or nothing. In such a world, the individual, as he tries to understand himself, finds no answer to what he is or what it is to be a subject. In Kierkegaard's words:

... nature, the totality of created things, is the work of God. And yet God is not there; but within the individual man there is potentiality (man is potentially spirit) which is awakened in inwardness to become a God relationship, and then it becomes possible to see God everywhere.[22]

Christianity is concerned with this subjectivity for its truth exists only in subjectivity, if it exists at all. Christianity has absolutely no existence in objectivity, and neither has the individual person. And thus the question is not whether to accept Christianity on the basis of its objective truth; that, for Kierkegaard, is paganism. The

21. Søren Kierkegaard, *Concluding An Unscientific Postscript*, [*Afsluttende Uvidenskabelig efterskrift (1846)*] translated by D. F. Swenson (Princeton, NJ: Princeton University Press, 1941), 182.
22. Ibid.

question is about the decision one makes in gaining faith, and since it is a pure decision, no objective considerations bear upon it. In other words, faith is not a matter of belief.

Another consideration is that the object of faith is not something belonging to this rational world. It is, rather, the absurd. Kierkegaard writes:

> Suppose [there is] a man who wishes to acquire faith; let the comedy begin. He wishes to have faith, but he wishes also to safeguard himself by means of an objective inquiry and its approximation process. What happens? With the help of the approximation process the absurd becomes something different: it becomes probable, it becomes increasingly probable, it becomes extremely and emphatically probable. Now he is ready to believe it and he ventures to claim for himself that he does not believe as shoemakers, tailors, and simple folk believe, but only after long deliberation. Now he is ready to believe it; and lo, now it has become precisely impossible to believe it. Anything that is almost probable, or probable, or extremely and emphatically probable, is something he can almost know—but it is impossible to believe. For the absurd is the object of faith, and the only object that can be believed.[23]

In other words, that which can be cashed into knowledge cannot be the object of faith. The object of faith is just that which cannot be a matter of belief in the sense of something which a little more evidence will make into knowledge.

Kierkegaard's idea of Christian faith has exercised a powerful influence on twentieth-century Protestant theology, notably on Karl Barth whose hostility to natural theology is reminiscent of that of Luther as well as Kierkegaard.

The line from Hume and to Kierkegaard wavers but nonetheless persists. Kant is convinced by Hume that there is no evidence for the existence of God, yet Kant affirms the reasonableness of belief.

---

23. Ibid., 189.

Then Hegel assumes, given the tenuousness of religious witness, that one of philosophy's primary tasks is the evaluation of the outlook provided by religion and its attendant theology, viewing it as a vague and uncertain preamble to philosophy. Finally Kierkegaard accepts the testimony of Christianity but finding no support for it in the natural order accepts it simply on faith. Faith for Kierkegaard is less a rational assent to an objective creed than a subjective commitment.

With respect to the role of religion in society, Kant is convinced of the importance of the visible church and Hegel of the cultural significance of religion. Both acknowledge the necessity of theology but reserve to philosophy the adjudication of its claims. Kierkegaard in contradistinction has little confidence in the detached rational analysis of Hegel or the propoedutic supplied by Kant and resorts instead to a Lutheran concept of belief. The dialogue as continued in the Anglo-Saxon world takes a new twist, and for that we look to John Stuart Mill in the nineteenth century and John Dewey in the twentieth.

MODERN INTERPRETATIONS

OF RELIGION, II

Mill, Marx, Dewey, Freud

It remains necessary to consider additional attitudes or theories of religion that gained widespread acceptance in the English-speaking world of the nineteenth and twentieth centuries. We begin with John Stuart Mill (1806–73), whose influence in the United States was pronounced. Equally important were the works of Marx and Freud. Mill was especially influential on the work of John Dewey, whose impact on the American educational system is enduring. Accepting the empiricist argument that there is no evidence for the existence of God, Mill and Dewey both address the question: "Given the reality of religion, is it useful to society, or is it, as Karl Marx asserted, an unmitigated evil, 'the opiate of the people'?"

Mill denied that there is evidence for the existence of God. However, his utilitarian conception of religion led him to affirm that we may without any affront to reason hope that the assurances religion offers may be true, and indeed, we should hope that they are, hoping that life is not so perishable as it seems, and that divine justice, though there is no sign of it in the world, may nevertheless be real. One may affirm a reality beyond the grave or one may deny it. From the standpoint of reason the two positions are an equal footing, being equally lacking in evidence. From the standpoint of utility, the former is uplifting, the latter conducive to a pessimism; the former energizing, the latter debilitating. Like all pessimisms, denial has a debilitating effect on one's character and energies. Hope in life eternal, on the contrary, provides the kind of attitude upon which many of the hard-won blessings of life and society have depended. Mill writes:

[I]t appears to me that the indulgences of hope with regard to the government of the universe and the destiny of man after death, while we recognize as a clear truth that we have no ground for more than a hope, is legitimate and philosophically defensible. The beneficial effect of such a hope is far from trifling.[1]

Mill, in his *Nature and Utility of Religion*,[2] puts to himself a number of questions: Whether belief in religion is indispensable to the temporal welfare of mankind; whether its usefulness is local and temporary; whether the benefits it yields might be obtained otherwise, without the very large alloy of evil, by which, even in the best form of belief, those benefits are qualified.

The value, therefore, of religion to the individual, both in the past and present, as a source of personal satisfaction and of elevated feelings, is not to be disputed. But it still has to be considered, whether in order to obtain this good, it is necessary to travel beyond the boundaries of the world we inhabit.[3] It is, in short, perfectly conceivable that religion may be morally useful without being intellectually sustainable.[4]

---

1. John Stuart Mill, *Theism* (Indianapolis: Bobbs-Merrill, 1957), 81.
2. John Stuart Mill, *Nature and Utility of Religion*, 3rd ed. (London; Longmans, 1885).
3. Ibid., 104–5.
4. Ibid., 74.

Mill cites Jeremy Bentham and Auguste Comte as his only two predecessors to interest themselves in the utility of religion. Religion, Mill argues, only seems powerful because when everyone believes, faith has a power.[5] Any institution that has the advantage of religion by inculcating its members from childhood is likely to produce social effects. Religious sanction, when not enforced by public opinion, produces scarcely any effect on conduct. Early education "possesses what is so much more difficult for later convictions to obtain—command over the feelings."[6]

Among the Greeks generally, social morality was not extremely dependent on religion. The worship of the gods was inculcated chiefly as a social duty, inasmuch as if they were neglected or insulted, it was believed that their displeasure would fall upon the state. Only when a morality is understood to come from the Gods, do men generally adopt it.[7]

In many respects Mill was merely a product of his age, unifying an outlook which had already gained acceptance among the intelligentsia. He represents the drift from an intrinsic consideration of the nature of religion, principally Christianity in its common tenets, to a quasi-sociological assessment of its worth viewed from the standpoint of the state. Auguste Comte, whom Mill considered a mentor and who for a time was materially supported by Mill, could not turn his back completely on the beneficent force of religion in the social order. Christianity permeated the whole of Europe, and even where it was not established, it provided the intellectual and moral support of many European institutions.

Yet ancient truths about nature, human nature, and cognitive ability had been successfully challenged by eighteenth- and nineteenth-century philosophers on both sides of the channel. Jean-

5. Ibid., 76, 81.   6. Ibid.
7. Ibid., 96

Jacques Rousseau (1712–78) was particularly influential not only in France, but in England and Germany as well. In his *Origin of Inequality* (1753), Rousseau attributes all the ills of man not to man's own sin or to ignorance but to social injustice and the corruptions of an artificial civilization. Rousseau in this and subsequent works pleads the cause of the individual against society, the poor against the rich, the common man against the privileged classes, the cause of love against convention, and the intuition of the religious mind against the orthodox philosopher and ecclesiastical authority.

Rousseau fired the minds of his generation with the ideal of democracy not merely as a system of government but as a new way of life, a vision of social justice and fraternity. With boundless optimism he preached a social idealism, a religion of humanity with a defined though simple body of dogma, designed to take the place of Christianity as the creed of a new age. His call for the complete reorganization of the social order became the creed of the French intelligentsia, a rationalized, humanitarian version of Christianity. Marx picked up the theme. If not in the marketplace, in the salons of the intelligentsia and in the academy atheism and agnosticism had carried the day. But Mill the empiricist and logician could not accept either theism or atheism as conclusively demonstrated. With Rousseau, Mill agreed that with the complete removal of belief in God the "religion of humanity" has the intrinsic capacity to fulfill all the functions of religion.

Distinguishing between "factual belief" and "imaginative hope," Mill held that in the realm of imagination and hope, a hypothesis can be entertained legitimately as long as it satisfies three conditions. It must be consistent with experience, internally coherent, and morally beneficial to mankind. The imaginative hope in acceptance of a finite God meets the three criteria, and experience teaches us that it is acceptable as well as morally useful. Imaginative hope in a finite God promotes good conduct and service to mankind. While there is no evidence for the existence of God, Mill sees nothing intrinsically inconceivable in the notion of an intelligent agent, superior to nature. Given the reality of evil, however, such an agent must be considered limited in power. He is not omnipotent. In effect, Mill affirms God's goodness at the expense of His power. Hope in the finite God has no meaning other than the pragmatic one of leading men to benevolence in the social order. Such an outlook, Mill is convinced, is compatible with Comte's positivism, which limits knowledge to the method of the natural sciences.

Christianity, Mill writes, has given us Christ as a standard of excellence.

. . . a model for imitation (that) is available even to the absolute unbeliever and can nevermore be lost to humanity. For it is Christ, rather than God, whom Christianity has held up to believers as the pattern of perfection for humanity. It is the God incarnate, more than the God of the Jews or of Nature, who being idealized, has taken so great and salutary hold on the modern mind. And what ever else may be taken away from us by rational criticism, Christ is still left.[8]

Such is the utility of Christianity, but from Mill's perspective, the religion of humanity is poised to offer other examples of figures to be emulated. For Mill's disciples in the twentieth century Albert Schweitzer (1875–1965) became a model of self-sacrifice. Another Disciple of Comte, Emile Durkheim, was not so positive in his assessment of religion. For Durkheim a major task of the state is to free individuals from partial societies, such as the family, religious organizations, and labor and professional groups. Ludwig Feuerbach (1804–72), whose materialism was to have a significant

8. Mill, *Theism*, 84.

influence on both Marx and Freud, went one step further, and assigned to reason the role of destroying the illusion of religion, "an illusion, however, which is by no means insignificant, but whose effect on mankind, rather, is utterly pernicious."[9] Freud took up the theme, and in his *Future of an Illusion* described the struggle of the scientific spirit against the "enemy" religion.[10]

In the United States, many of these ideas were to find twentieth-century expression in the writings of John Dewey. In his theory of education Dewey provided no place for religion or for religious institutions, no matter what roles they may have played in the past. Religion, he thought, is an unreliable source for knowledge and motivation, in spite of contentions to the contrary. He admitted that many of the values held dear by the religious are worthy of consideration and should not be abandoned, but argued that a proper rationale ought to be sought for those deemed commendable. Through his critique of religion, Dewey sought not merely to eliminate the church from political influence but to eliminate it as an effective agent even in private life. Religion, he taught, was socially dangerous insofar as it gives practical credence to a divine law and attempts to mold personal or social conduct in conformity with norms that look beyond and therefore neglect temporal society.[11]

We have come a long way from Kant's appreciation of religion as a moral tutor and Hegel's appreciation of its cultural signifi-

9. Cf. Karl Löwith, *From Hegel to Nietzsche,* translated by D. E. Green (New York: Holt Rinehart and Winston, 1964), for a discussion of the course of nineteenth-century thought on the role of religion.

10. *The Future of an Illusion: Basic Writings of Sigmund Freud,* edited by A. H. Brill (New York: Modern Library, 1938).

11. Of the many works of John Dewey three may be taken as setting forth his philosophy in outline: *Experience and Nature* (Chicago: Open Court, 1925), *Theory of Valuation* (Chicago: University of Chicago Press, 1939), and *Reconstruction in Philosophy* (New York: New American Library, 1939).

cance. Others could be taken as examples of a secular outlook at war with religion, but given their influence Marx and Dewey are difficult to ignore and are prime examples of the march to a secular humanism.

Karl Heinrich Marx (1818–83) and John Dewey (1859–1952) both represent a secular humanism that they not only helped define but promoted from its intellectual roots to an active political and social program. Even a cursory examination of their work discloses the close connection between theory and praxis in this case between a theory of religion and a social program.

With respect to his views on religion, Karl Marx was greatly influenced by Hegel but also by theologians and biblical scholars such as David Strauss (1808–74) and Bruno Bauer (1808–82).[12] From Hegel he accepted the notion that religion was a comprehensive account of human existence, somewhat more refined and precise than the ambiguous conception allowable to the poet but lacking the rigor and precision that only philosophy can provide. This perception of the quasi-poetic nature of religion was reinforced by Strauss and Bauer, who showed Marx how to understand biblical literature. In the 1830's, when this idea was relatively new, Strauss and Bauer convinced Marx that the Sacred Scriptures were simply a work of the human imagination. The message of the Scriptures is wholly metaphorical; it is merely an imaginative expression of

---

12. David Strauss (1808–74) in his first major work, *Das Leben Jesu, kritisch bearbeitet* (2 vols., 1835–36; *The Life of Jesus, Critically Examined,* 1846), denied the historical value of the Christian Gospels as historical myths, unintentionally created, the embodiment of the primitive hopes of the early Christian community. Shortly before the end of his life, he published *Der alte und neue Glaube* (1872), *The Old Earth and The New* (1873), in which he ventured to replace Christianity with a Darwinian-influenced "scientific materialism." Bruno Bauer (1808–82) similarly concluded that the Gospels were a record not of history but of human fantasies. Marx, when a student in Berlin, enrolled in one of Bauer's courses on the prophet Isaiah.

men's moral ideas. Strauss and Bauer agreed with Hegel that the biblical God is only an imaginative way of looking at the Absolute. Accordingly, they were convinced that we must move beyond the traditional notion of God and recognize that religion is merely one way of portraying the relationship between man and his moral ideas. Feuêrbach would add that this is an imperfect way, since religion puts moral ideas into a separate and distant realm. The task, says Feuêrbach, is to recover the purely human meaning of religion. We have to bring religion back to its proper proportions as an expression of human moral aspirations.

In his highly influential work, *Das Wesen des Christentum*,[13] Feuêrbach denied the supernatural and everything in religion not of a naturalistic and human origin. Feuêrbach had systematically translated all statements about God into statements about man. The word "God," Feuêrbach maintains, is but a designation for man's highest aspirations, a changing "ideal" that men establish for themselves. In the person of God, man celebrates his own personality in its limitless strivings. Put crudely, since the political and economic life of man is incapable of fulfilling his true self, he creates the illusory world of religion and its promise of eternal fulfillment.

In the eyes of the young Hegelians of whom Marx was one, Feuêrbach appeared to have demolished Christianity and with it the social and political institutions grounded upon it. In doing so he prepared the way for a humanism freed from traditional moral and social constraints. This teaching was to leave its mark on a company of men who played an important role in the shaping of the modern mind, including Nietzsche, Scheler, Freud, Sartre, Fromm, and Dewey. Feuêrbach aimed to change the friends of God into friends of man, worshipers into workers, believers into

13. Ludwig Feuêrbach, *Das Wesen des Christentum* (1854), translated as *The Essence of Christianity* by George Eliot (New York: Harper & Row, 1957).

thinkers. Anthropology would replace theology, politics, and religion.

It is in this context that Marx will say of religion that it is man's self-administered opiate. Inasmuch as religion prevents man from seeking happiness when it can be found in this life it must be attacked, and not merely at the theoretical level but in action. We cannot change society for the good simply by philosophizing about it; we must act. Philosophy must leave the plane of theory and with the help of the intellectual class penetrate the masses. It must culminate in social revolution, a revolution of the proletariat against the established order.

Marx was in strong agreement with Feuêrbach. He declared, "For Germany, the criticism of religion is in the main complete, and criticism of religion is the premise of all criticism."[14] From now on the criticism of religion would be translated into criticism of politics and the social order. Marx fully accepted the current secular understanding of religion and did not wish to redo the work of Hegel, Strauss, Bauer, and Feuêrbach. He thought it important, however, to add one note. Feuêrbach had been extremely vague about the reason why men tend to project their ideas into the objective order or tend to personify them in God. Marx concluded that because of intolerable social conditions engendered by a capitalist economy, people were forced to project their moral ideal into an afterworld.

This addition gives a more precise meaning to Marx's concept of religion. In his essay on Hegel, Marx calls religion the theoretical counterpart to private property. He uses the phrase, "the perverted consciousness of a perverted world." In the practical order we have the inhuman capitalist system which in the theoretical or-

14. Karl Marx, "Contribution to the Critique of Hegel's Philosophy of Law: Introduction" in Karl Marx and Friedrich Engels, *Collected Works* (New York: International Publishers, 1976), Vol. 3, 175.

der has created the myths of religion to console the unfortunate. Thus we have Marx's famous dictum, A[Religion] is the opiate of the people." The best way to break the habit of religious reference is not to attack it head on but to attack the practical conditions that engender the religious ideal. The true abolition of religion will occur automatically as a byproduct of changing economics and social structures. Eventually, religion will wither away as capitalism withers away. Marx wrote:

To be radical is to grasp things by the root. But for man the root is man himself. . . . The criticism of religion ends with the doctrine that man is the supreme being for man. It ends therefore with the categorical imperative to overthrow all those conditions in which man is an abased, enslaved, abandoned, contemptible being.[15]

If man and his world are self-created, then man cannot and should not expect to be liberated from his sufferings by some superhuman force—good or evil—but must set about freeing himself. In other words, belief in self-creation implies that one must also accept the idea of self-emancipation. The proletariat, in liberating the whole of mankind, can liberate itself as a class. This is the foundation of Marx's socialism. The struggle for fulfillment demands a militant humanism, with a goal nothing less than the formation of a classless society. The goal is projected not merely for German society but for mankind in general. Struggle is unavoidable. Marx is not hesitant to enlist hatred of the enemy in the name of love of neighbor: this is a contradiction only if one does not see beyond the surface. The humanist, says Marx, must approach the problem of love not abstractly but in a concrete way. He enjoins actions to frustrate and render harmless all those who, for the sake of their private interests, bar man's way to happiness. For in a soci-

15. Ibid., 182.

ety demarcated by class, they are enemies of mankind, whether their behavior is conscious or unconscious. Anyone who understands this must also realize that the enemies of brotherly love—enemies of the cause of humanity—must be fought actively, and this is inseparably connected with feelings of hate. Love of mankind, far from excluding hatred of those who act objectively in the name of the oppressed, in fact presupposes it.

Another student of Hegel and Feuêrbach, John Dewey (1859–1952), taught for more than half a century in three major universities and played a critical role in the training of public-school teachers in the United States. The longest part of Dewey's teaching career was spent at Columbia University, with which he was associated for forty-seven years and where he worked actively as a teacher for twenty-five. Dewey transmitted his views to educators who wrote the manuals that were used in teachers' colleges throughout the country. The evangelical character of his philosophy, with its emphasis on utility, change, progress, and the future rather than the past, caught on and became the standard American credo.

The core of Dewey's philosophy of religion can be found in a small book he produced near the end of his teaching career, *A Common Faith*.[16] Dewey opens the book with the observation that throughout history men have been divided into two camps over the question of religion. The focal point of this division is, in his view, the reality of "the supernatural,"[17] its affirmation and its denial. Religionists maintain that no belief can be genuinely called religious which is not connected with the supernatural. Among believers there is a range of positions, from those of the Greek and Roman churches who hold that their dogmatic and sacramental

16. John Dewey, *A Common Faith* (New Haven: Yale University Press, 1934), 1–3
17. Ibid.

systems are the only sure means of access to the supernatural, to the nondoctrinal theist or mild deist. Also in this spectrum are many Protestant persuasions which consider Scripture and conscience to be adequate avenues to religious truth. Those who are opposed to religion believe that the advance of anthropological and psychological studies has adequately revealed the all-too-human sources of what has customarily been ascribed to the supernatural. The extremists in this group believe that with the elimination of belief in the supernatural not only historical religions but everything of a religious nature must be dismissed.

Having appraised the situation, Dewey sets out to examine the root cause of the division among men over the issue of religion. He attempts to determine the reasons for the identification of the religious with the supernatural and its ensuing consequences. In so doing, he offers another conception of the nature of the religious experience, one that separates it from the supernatural and its derivations. Removing these, in his view, will enable genuinely religious human experience to develop freely on its own account. To this end, in the first of the three chapters comprising *A Common Faith*, Dewey introduces a distinction between the noun "religion" and the adjective "religious." This distinction provides a herme-neutical tool for salvaging that which is valid in "religious" experiences and freeing it from the encumbrances resulting from efforts of various historical religions to explain those experiences. There is, in Dewey's estimation, a validity to what is globally designated as religious experience. Yet this can be had apart from historical religions, which have in fact hampered the full import of such experiences.[18] If this valid core can be brought to light, then men will stop thinking that they need religions to have religious experience.

18. Ibid.

Dewey acknowledges that religion plays a part in the lives of most men. When fully embraced, it can modify one's attitude to life in a significant and enduring way. In the face of adversity, religion can inspire a sense of peace and security; in a period of change, it can help one to adjust and adapt. Unifying the diverse elements of experience, it can produce a vision that entails a voluntary submission to reality, not in stoic acceptance of what cannot be changed but through an interior redirection of will and attitude.[19]

While Dewey does not deny that a religious attitude has these and many other benefits, he does deny that these effects are peculiar to religion. Religions claim to bring about a change in attitude, yet institutions use these attitudes to create established churches, thereby changing moral faith into speculative faith and dogma. Moral faith entails the conviction that some spiritual end should be supreme over one's conduct; speculative faith, by contrast, attributes existence to that end, objectifying it and making it a truth for the intellect. Moral faith subordinates itself to an end that asserts a rightful claim over one's desires and purposes. It is practical, not intellectual. And while it goes beyond evidence, it has only the authority of a freely admitted ideal, not that of a fact. Institutional religions take this attitude, give objective reality to what was a moral ideal, and present it as the final reality at the heart of everything that exists. Religion has no difficulty in doing this, for desire has a powerful influence on intellectual beliefs. Men tend to believe what they ardently desire to be the case. At any rate, it is always easier to believe that the ideal is already a fact than to strive to make it so.[20]

Dewey regards the ideal of moral faith as fundamentally more

19. Ibid., 16–17.
20. Ibid., 22.

religious than its reification in formal religions, for the ideal points to possibilities and all human endeavor is better motivated by faith in what is possible than by adherence to what is already actual. Furthermore, such an ideal can be denotive of activity on the natural level. It is consonant with nature and does not divorce us from it. He states, "Faith in the continued disclosing of truth through directed cooperative human endeavor is more religious in quality than is any faith in a completed revelation." Thus, nature and man's experience in it become both the source and object of the ideal that directs life. Any activity pursued on behalf of an ideal end is religious in nature. The essentially irreligious attitude is that which attributes human achievement and purpose to man in isolation from nature and his fellow men. To regard the religious act in this way is to avoid the antagonism between religion and modern science:

The positive lesson is that religious qualities and values, if they are real at all, are not bound up with any single item of intellectual assent, not even that of the existence of the God of theism; and that under existing conditions, the religious function in experience can be emancipated only through surrender of the whole notion of special truths that are religious by their own nature, together with the idea of peculiar avenues of access to such truths. For were we to admit that there is but one method for ascertaining fact and truth—that conveyed by the word "scientific" in its most general and generous sense—no discovery in any branch of knowledge and inquiry could then disturb the faith that is religious.[21]

It is worth noting that Dewey takes leave of William James's pragmatic approach to religious belief. James had been willing to grant some validity and meaning to a belief that produced satisfactory results in the life of the believer. Dewey is more cautious. He asks whether James employs the pragmatic method to discover

21. Ibid., 32–33.

value in the consequences of some religious formula that has its logical content already fixed or uses his pragmatic method to criticize, revise, and, ultimately, constitute the meaning of the formula.[22] Dewey is afraid lest some may understand pragmatism in the first sense and be disposed to attribute existential value to fixed dogmas that science has rendered untenable. If pragmatism is of any value in the religious sphere, its contribution is to replace faith in the supernatural order found in traditional religion with faith in the religious possibilities found in ordinary experience. There can be faith in intelligence, a devotion to the process by which truth is discovered, which would include a commitment both to science and to the worth and dignity of man. In this way, morality and religion will become an integral part of everyday living, emerging out of nature and renovating the nature out of which it has arisen.

The ideal ends to which we attach our faith are not shadowy and wavering. They assume concrete form in our understanding of our relations to one another and the values contained in these relations. We who now live are parts of a humanity that has reacted with nature. The things in civilization we most prize are not of ourselves. They exist by grace of the doings and sufferings of the continuous human community in which we are a link.[23]

Although Dewey's naturalism rules out a God who is responsible for the creation and governance of the universe, he nevertheless attempts to understand the concept "God," its origin and function. In this effort his work is not unlike that of Feuêrbach, though it is not certain that Dewey ever read *The Essence of Christianity.* Putting the question to himself, "Are the ideals which move us genuinely ideal, or are they ideal only in contrast with our present es-

---

22. See also Dewey's *Essays in Experimental Logic* (Chicago: University of Chicago Press, 1916), 313.

23. Dewey, *Faith,* 87.

tate?", he replies that the answer determines the meaning of the word "God." For Dewey the word "God" denotes the unity of all the ideal ends arousing us to desire and action.[24]

According to Dewey, the origin of the traditional notion of God is easy enough to explain. There has always been in human nature a tendency to attribute prior existence to the objects of desire. Qualities are discovered in nature; goods are grouped in experience. Physical and psychological tendencies and activities are observed. These become entwined and united in human emotion and activity. It is not at all surprising that they should be thought to have a unified existence in their perfect state apart from the conditions under which we find them in experience.

To re-separate the various qualities may, indeed, be a difficult task, but the benefits to be derived from such an effort are many. In the first place, such a separation will free the religious attitude from tenets that are daily becoming more dubious. Witness the doubt which discoveries in geology and astronomy have cast on the doctrine of Creation, the findings in modern biology which have rendered ancient conceptions of soul and body obsolete, and the explanations in psychology for what were once understood to be supernatural phenomena.

There is another inherent difficulty with the search for a personal God. Such an inquiry necessarily diverts man's attention and energy away from ideal values and the conditions by which they may be promoted. To the extent that we argue about the existence of God, we choose to spend valuable time on something from which no good can come in preference to devoting that time to more fruitful enterprises. History has shown that men have never fully used their power to advance the good life as long as they have waited upon some extrinsic power to remedy the situation for them.

24. Ibid., 42.

Such an attitude necessarily neglects the value intrinsic to the natural order. It leaves the world alone and seeks a solution for difficulty elsewhere. It substitutes personal prayer for cooperative effort.

If, on the other hand, we do not identify the ideal as a reified personal being, then this ideal may be thought of as being grounded in natural conditions. The ideal emerges as man's imagination idealizes existence with respect to the possibilities offered by thought and action.

There are values, goods, actually realized upon a natural basis—the goods of human association, of art and knowledge. The idealizing imagination seizes upon the most precious things found in the climacteric moments of experience and projects them. We need no external criterion and guarantee for their goodness. They are had, they exist as good, and out of them we frame our ideal ends.[25]

It is also true that these ideals do in a sense exist. They direct our actions and exist in the conditions that prompt their fulfillment. With a new ideal end, a new vision emerges and familiar objects are seen in new relations as they serve that end. As these values and ideals are dwelt upon and tested by practice, they are purified and strengthened. The values become more definitive and coherent and so have greater effect upon present conditions.

Values and situations modify each other. We have neither ideals that are completely embodied in existence nor ideals that are merely rootless fancies. This active relation between the ideal and actual is what Dewey calls "God." By so conceiving God, he seeks to make man a citizen of earth and to restore him to the fatherland in which he has his roots and his destiny.

This concept of God encompasses all the possibilities that nature exhibits. These possibilities beckon each and every man. They

25. Ibid., 80.

point to the possibility of a fuller and more perfect reality as a result of action aimed at bettering the natural situation. They are perceived by the imagination, clarified by the method of science, and tested and modified by experience. Thus reshaped and purified, they in turn shape and purify the activity which they inspire.

Criticizing the traditional idea of God, Dewey cannot see how a God who exists apart from the universe can in any way be a God for man. To direct man to believe in such a God is to dehumanize and denaturalize him. Dewey thought that even the Absolute Mind of Hegel, immanent in nature, denied the reality of the finite and the natural.

In the final chapter of *A Common Faith,* Dewey addresses what he calls "The Human Abode of the Religious Function." There he observes that the core of religion has generally been found in rites and ceremonies. But given the secular character of our present society, few persons can understand, without the use of imagination, what it means socially for a religion to permeate all the customs and activities of group life. Since the Renaissance there has been a shift in the social center of gravity from the sacred to the secular. Today the conditions under which people meet and act together are thoroughly secular. Interests and values are neither derived from nor related to the church. Religion is a matter of personal choice and not a matter of social order.

This is not to be regretted, however. When religion was grounded in the supernatural, a sharp line between the religious and the secular prevailed. In Dewey's view religion necessitates no such division, for when the religious function is emancipated from religion, the distinction between the sacred and the secular fades. Protestantism has rightly emphasized the fact that the relation of man to God is primarily an individual matter, a matter of personal choice and responsibility. Beliefs and rites that make the relation between man and God a collective and institutional affair erect barriers between the human soul and the divine spirit. When primacy is given to the direct relation of the conscience and will to God, religion is placed on its only real and solid foundation. Social change is better accomplished through the common effort of men and women than through any institutional effort. Contrary to a popular misperception, Dewey argues that the secularization of society has not been accompanied by increasing degeneration. Rather it is the forces that are independent of organized religion that have worked to enhance human relations and have resulted in intellectual and aesthetic development. In fact, the churches have lagged behind in most social movements.

Dewey is convinced that a depreciation of natural social values results from a comparison with a supernatural source. The objection to supernaturalism is that it stands in the way of an effective realization of the sweep and depth of the implications of natural human relations. "It stands in the way of using the means that are in our power to make radical changes in these relations."[26]

Although Dewey discounts religion as the "only finally dependable source of motivation," he would, nevertheless have the churches show a more active interest in social affairs. But they would have to do so on equal footing with other institutions. This participation would require their surrender of any claims to an exclusive and authoritative position.

Secular interests and activities have grown up outside of organized religions and are independent of their authority. The hold of these interests upon the thoughts and desires of men has cowed the social importance of organized religions into a corner and the area of this corner is decreasing.[27]

26. Ibid., 80.
27. Ibid., 83.

Dewey suggests that thoughtful persons should work to emancipate the religious quality of experience from the accretions that have grown up about it and that limit its credibility and influence. Philosophers should develop and make explicit those principles and values inherent in civilization to which the race is heir, values that are inherent in the continuous human community of which the present generation is but a link. In these are contained all the elements for a religious faith that is not confined to sect, class, or race. "Such a faith has always been implicitly the common faith of mankind. It remains to make it explicit and militant."[28]

Democracy as understood by Dewey does not refer to a system of balloting. Nor is it a government with checks and balances intended to prevent the majority from running roughshod over the rights of a minority. Rather it is a method for dissolving majorities and minorities; it is a way of conceptually resolving differences. The majority must give up its claim to truth, correctness, or rightness in the face of serious challenge. Numerical strength does not provide a warrant. Unrestrained legislation that favors one point of view is not justified by the fact that an overwhelming majority shares that viewpoint as long as a minority exists with different opinions.

Democracy calls for compromise, conceptually and practically. Between affirmation and negation lies the "truth." The truth is not simply the expedient, nor is it to be anchored in an historically given constitution. A constitution is itself not strictly an immutable document; it must be interpreted in the light of contemporary circumstances. Appeals to a Christian past, to a Christian heritage, to a Christian rationale for our present law are not to be admitted. Problems have to be resolved in the present con-

28. Ibid., 87.

text. Our forebears have no hold on us. Like Marx, Dewey's purely naturalistic account of religion has social and political consequences.

We turn now to another important nineteenth-twentieth-century figure, Sigmund Freud (1856–1939), who, with Marx, Nietzsche, and Feuêrbach provides a genetic description of how the idea of "God" was formed. In common, they hold that God is a purely subjective product of our human miseries, aspirations, and search after power. Freud takes seriously the supposed conflict between inherited religion and science. In his *New Introductory Lecture on Psychoanalysis,*[29] he contrasts what he calls the religious *Weltanschauung* with the scientific *Weltanschauung.* In his description of the religious world-view, Freud characterizes the intellectual emotion and moral life of man in relationship to God in this way:

If we are to give an account of the grandiose nature of religion, we must bear in mind what it undertakes to do for human beings. It gives them information about the origin and coming into existence of the universe, it assures them of its protection and ultimate happiness in the ups and downs of life and it directs their thoughts and actions by the precepts which it lays down with its whole authority.[30]

In contrast to the religious world-view, the scientific world-view has but one basic presupposition. This, he writes, is that "there are no sources of knowledge of the universe other than the intellectual working over of carefully scrutinized observations . . .

29. Sigmund Freud, *Neue Folge der Vovlesungen zur Einführung indie Psychoanalyse,* translated as *New Introductory Lecture on Psychoanalysis,* and edited by James Strackey (London: Hogarth Press, 1964), Vol. 22, 161.

30. Sigmund Freud, *Complete Psychological Works,* edited by James Strackey (London: Hogarth Press, 1964), Vol. 22, 161.

and alongside of it no knowledge derived from revelation, intuition, or divination."³¹

The conflict between the two world views comes precisely at this point for religion in satisfying man's desire for knowledge, according to Freud, "does the same thing that science attempts to do with its means, and at the point enters into rivalry with it."³² There is no basic conflict between these two world views with reference to certain other religious claims. Insofar as religion has the power to comfort in the face of the vicissitudes of life, science is no match for religion.

Convinced of the falsity of belief in the existence of God, Freud explains the origin of the religious world-view in these words:

This remarkable combination in religion of instruction, consolation, and requirements can only be understood if it is subject to genetic analysis. This may be approached from the most striking point of the aggregate, from its instruction on the origin of the universe. . . . The doctrine is . . . that the universe was created by a being resembling a man, but magnificent in every respect. . . . It is an interesting fact that this creator is always only a single being. . . . It is interesting, too, that the creator is usually a man. Our further path is made easy to recognize, for this god-creator is undisguisedly called "father." Psychoanalysis infers that he really is the father, worth all the magnificence in which he once appeared to the small child. A religious man pictures the creation of the universe just as he pictures his own origin.³³

This is the heart of Freud's position on religion. The psychological basis of the belief in the existence of God lies in our leftover childhood needs and fantasies. This theory of neurotic projection is not only able to give an account of the origin of illusory belief in the existence of God but it is also able to give an account of the other two religious claims as well. It is this same father who pro-

31. Ibid., 159.   32. Ibid., 161.
33. Ibid., 162–63.

tected and watched over the small helpless child, who, as the grown man, having expanded his childhood parental image to cosmic proportions, looks, in his adult helplessness, to the illusory God. God the Father replaces the earthly father as an image for protection and final happiness. Thus the psychological basis for the second religious claim for man. "It is also the same parent who taught the little child what it might and might not do, made him accept certain limitations, rewarded his goodness and punished his wickedness. This childhood behavioral framework is carried over to the cosmic God-Father image and now this illusory God-Father becomes the authority for the adult's moral guides to action. Thus the psychological basis for the third religious claim for man: Their parents' prohibitions and demands persist with them as moral conscience."[34]

It must be said that Freud's cultural and psychoanalytic report on the birth of the idea of God has no explanatory relevance to the question of God's existence. Kant rightly locates the question of our knowledge of God's existence on the plane of judgment and inference, even though he finds no way of resolving it.

To bring this section to a close, we must conclude that if there is a logic to religion, there is a logic to irreligion. Wherever Marxists or secular humanists have achieved political ascendancy, religious education, if not worship itself, is suppressed. The cultural revolutions effected under Marxist regimes in the Soviet Union, China, and smaller countries like Cuba are well known. Less obvious is the triumph of secular humanism in the United States and the cultural revolution which followed, where in the span of a half-century we have witnessed the collapse of traditional morality, and the widespread acceptance of deviant sexual practice, which nineteenth-century critics of religion would themselves have abhorred.

34. Ibid., 164.

Absent belief in the existence of God, religion, as Marx predicted, has withered. The roots of agnosticism and atheism we have seen are metaphysical. If there is no evidence for the existence of God, faith becomes an option; no matter that it may be regarded as rational choice, it is still a choice and one with repercussions in the moral order. History teaches that morality or its absence soon determines social and political policy. Cultural differences emerge between societies that cultivate the recognition of and homage to an all-knowing and powerful God and those that don't.

This examination necessarily moves from consideration of the role of religion in society to a discussion of the relation between church and state. Only then do we see the logic of religion fully played out as bodies politic collectively assert their perception of the relation of man to God. "The West" and "Christendom" were terms once used interchangeably. Since the nineteenth century that identification has been rendered dubious as the Enlightenment critiques undermine Christianity's confidence in itself.

The founding of the American republic in the late eighteenth century offers a case study of men of good will who, coming from diverse intellectual backgrounds—deist, Protestant, and Catholic—sought to establish a proper relationship between the churches and the federal government. As yet largely untouched by the Enlightenment, the Founding Fathers were convinced of the importance of worship and of the moral discipline which only religion can impose. Their convictions remained the rule of law until the U.S. Supreme Court, in a series of decisions beginning in 1947, began to interpret the U.S. Constitution in a manner was ultimately to remove religion as a moral and cultural guide, leading John Neuhaus to lament "the naked public square."

VII

RELIGION AND THE STATE IN
WESTERN DEMOCRACIES

Jacques Maritain

Throughout the course of Western history, kings, princes, and statesmen as well as philosophers have recognized the importance of the unity of thought among the peoples subject to rule. To preserve its very being, it has been thought the state must preserve that which bonds the people and makes a nation possible. Almost without exception, until the rise of nationalism in recent centuries it has been religion which has provided the common *Weltangschuung*. Atheism was condemned by Plato. In ancient Greece heresy was often regarded as a capital offense. The religious deviant was regarded as a threat to the state. Christ himself was put to death because of his unorthodox teaching. Christians were persecuted by the Romans. From Roman times, kings and emperors determined the religion of their peoples. Constantine established Christianity as the official religion of the realm and consequently of the West. With the dividing of Christendom, Protestantism in one form or another replaced Catholicism as the state religion in northern Europe. In recent times socialist regimes, whenever they come to power, in the interest of their supporting ideology, suppressed religious education if not religion itself. The iconoclast movement following the Reformation and the desecration of churches in modern European history from Napoleonic times to the present is but one facet of an attempt to suppress an inherited Christianity. Soviet suppression of religion is well known. In North America, the secular state is less overt in its antagonism to religion but nevertheless handicaps religious education, and the United States has even removed references to God and to biblical moral teaching from the state schools.

This leads to the question: "What is the role of religion in society? What should be the attitude of the state toward religion." Does the state have a stake in the religious education and moral bearing of the populace? If not, from whence is the necessary intellectual and moral unity indispensable for the rule of law to arise?

The founders of the American republic wrestled with these questions of establishment. At the time of the American founding, nine of the thirteen colonies had established churches, but the new republic in the First Amendment to the U.S. Constitution proclaimed that "Congress shall make no law regarding the establishment of religion or prohibit the free exercise thereof." The debate between John Adams and Thomas Jefferson on establishment is instructive, insofar as it graphically illustrates two conceptions of the role of religion in society. Jefferson argued that the state should give no special aid, support, or privilege to any religion. The state should predicate no laws or policies on explicitly religious grounds. No one form of Christianity nor Christianity itself should be supported by the state to the exclusion of other religions. All forms of Christianity should stand on their own feet and on equal footing with the faiths of Jews and Mohammedans. Their survival must depend on the cogency of their word.[1]

Adams recognized that every civil society must countenance a

---

1. Thomas Jefferson Autobiography (1821) in Padover, ed., *The Complete Jefferson*, 1147.

plurality of forms of religious association and practice. The notion that it is possible for the state to coerce all persons into adherence to a common public religion is for Adams a "philosophical fiction." Persons make their own judgments in matters of faith, for the rights of conscience are "indisputable, inalienable, indefeasible, and divine." The maintenance of religious pluralism is essential for the protection of religion itself and other forms of liberty.[2]

Adams, nevertheless thought it necessary to acknowledge a "public religion." Every polity must establish by law some form of public religion, some image and ideal of itself, some common values and beliefs to undergird and support the plurality of religions. The notion that a state and society can remain neutral and purged of any religion is, for Adams, unthinkable. Absent a commonly adopted set of values, politicians will inevitably set out their private convictions as public ones. In Adams's view, the creed of this public religion is honesty, diligence, devotion, obedience, virtue, and love of God, neighbor, and self. Its expression is to be found in the Bible, in the Constitution, and in the memorials of patriots. Its liturgy, he thought, is the public proclamations of oaths, prayers, songs, and Thanksgiving Day ceremonies. In a letter to Benjamin Rush, Adams writes:

The only foundation of a free constitution is pure virtue. . . . I agree with you in sentiment that religion and virtue are the only foundations not only of republicanism and all free government but of social felicity. . . . The Bible contains the most profound philosophy, the most perfect morality and the most refined policy that ever was conceived upon earth.[3]

2. Letters to Abigail Adams, June 21, 1776, in Adams, ed. Works, Vol. 4, 194. *The Works of John Adams,* 10 vols., ed. J. F. Adams, (Boston: Little, Brown, 1850–56).

3. *The Spur of Fame: Dialogues of John Adams and Benjamin Rush, 1805–13,* edited by John A. Schutz and Douglas Adair (San Marino, CA: Huntington Library, 1966), 75–76, as quoted by John Witte, Jr., "A Most Mild and Equitable Establishment of Religion: John Adams and the Massachusetts Experiment," in *Journal of Church and State,* Vol. 41, Spring 1999, 216.

Adams was not alone in favoring some sort of establishment. In eighteenth-century England at the time of the American founding, establishment was seen as the primary means of providing the unity of outlook necessary for the preservation of the realm. John Locke, David Hume, and Adam Smith favored establishment.

Adams was delegated by the drafting committee of what eventually became the Massachusetts Constitution to prepare the first draft for debate by the state Constitutional Convention of 1780. Article III of that draft expressed his personal conviction:

Good morals, being necessary for the preservation of civil society, and the knowledge and belief of the being of GOD [Adams's caps], His providential government of the world and a future state of rewards and punishment, being the only true foundation of morality, the legislature hath, therefore, a right, and ought to provide at the expense of the subject, if necessary, a suitable support for the public worship of GOD, and the teachers of religion and morals. . . . All monies, paid by the subject of public worship, and of the instructors in religion and morals, shall if he requires it, be uniformly applied to the support of the teacher or teachers of his own religious denomination. . . .[4]

Adams feared that a failure to acknowledge the public utility of religion would allow secular prejudice to become the state prerogative. Adams was indeed prescient. Failure to accord religion equal footing in the allocation of educational support has led in effect to the establishment of a secular ideology. In a series of decisions since 1947, the Supreme Court of the United States has denied parents the benefit of their tax dollars if they choose to educate their children in the light of their religious faith. Adams would be aghast at this use of the separation metaphor, a metaphor coined by Jefferson in a letter to the Danbury Baptists (January 1, 1802), to exclude prayer and the posting of the Ten Commandments from the

4. Adams, J. F., *Works*, Vol. 4, 221–22.

state schools. "Congress shall make no law respecting the establishment of religion" has been used to create "a wall of separation between Church and state" disregarding the second clause which does not "prohibit(s) the free exercise thereof." The concept of "procedural democracy" now regnant in academic circles denies the ability of the state to choose between competing conceptions of the good. Procedural democracy rests upon the assumption that there is no way to determine the common good. The state in adopting its policies is not to draw upon any one moral tradition, and certainly not a religious tradition. Religion is a purely private or subjective affair, not a trustworthy source of principles applicable to public policy. Unfortunately, with the dismissal of religion often goes that other support of republican government, the classical learning which informed the political philosophy of the founding fathers. At the time of the American founding, Cicero's discourses framed the issues which were addressed in the Declaration of Independence and the Constitution, topics such as liberty, the nature and source of law, the common good, security, patriotism, toleration, and the role of religion in society. Eighteenth-century readers understood Cicero to be a defender of rectitude, virtue, and conservative customs, and of the indispensable role that religion plays in fostering these values. A reflection of this view is manifest in the writings of Adams. For Cicero, the highest aim of the ruler is the security and welfare of the community because the common welfare is the indispensable condition for personal advancement. Security may be the highest aim, but the maintenance of morality in the populace is also a fundamental responsibility of the ruler.

The procedural democracy that denies the ruler the ability to distinguish between what is truly good and what is merely expedient is the fruit of an optimistic liberal creed which set out to refashion the world in the nineteenth century. This liberal creed plays somewhat the same part in Western nations as that played by Christianity in other periods of Western history. It reinforces Adams's judgment that every living culture must possess some spiritual dynamic which provides the energy necessary for the sustained social effort which constitutes civilization. That creed found its definitive expression in a late work by John Dewey, *A Common Faith*, already discussed.

The contemporary situation is a far cry from that represented by the spokesman for the colonists, who took for granted the good effects of religion. While John Adams argued for "the establishment" of public religion in Massachusetts, James Madison took a similar position in Virginia. His counterpart, George Mason, in drafting the Virginia Bill of Rights, provided that men should enjoy "the fullest toleration in the exercise of religion."[5]

His colleague, James Madison, thought stronger language was needed since toleration could be taken to mean only a limited form of religious liberty, i.e., the toleration of dissenters in a state where there was an established religion. Madison drafted a substitute, declaring that "all men are equally entitled to the full and free exercise of religion" and therefore, "that no man or class of men ought on account of religion to be invested with any peculiar emoluments or privileges."[6] Madison was writing in a state that did in fact have an established church, and it was not his intent to disestablish the Anglican Church in Virginia. Thus, Virginia was permitted to retain her established church, and dissenters were guaranteed tolerance. Out of the Virginia debate came the adoption of the First Amendment to the United States Constitution with its declaration that Congress shall make "no law respecting an establishment of religion or prohibiting the free exercise thereof."

5. *The Papers of George Mason, 1725–1791*, edited by Robert A. Rutland (Chapel Hill, NC: University of North Carolina Press, 1970), Vol. 1, 278.

6. *The Papers of James Madison*, edited by William T. Hutchinson and William M.E. Rachals (Chicago: University of Chicago Press, 1962), Vol. 1, 174.

It is only within the past fifty years that the United States Supreme Court has produced a significant gloss on the Constitution's
First Amendment.[7] In those fifty years the neutrality doctrine,
which governed legislation and the courts in the early days of the
Republic, came to be construed not simply as neutrality between
sects but a neutrality between religion and irreligion. Legislation
affecting religion, the court came to hold, must have a secular purpose and a primary effect that neither advances nor inhibits religion. While Justice William Douglas in the Zorach decision (1952)
may have reflected the sentiment of the court when he wrote, "We
are a religious people whose institutions presuppose a Supreme
Being," before his death he was to emerge as a spokesman for an
entirely different doctrine, namely, that of benevolent neutrality
which affirms that the state does not have a stake in the success of
religion. Such a turn might have surprised Jefferson who, while he
spoke of "a wall of separation," never wanted to divorce religion
from public life. Like Hobbes and Locke he believed in the social
utility of religion. Commonly held religious beliefs are necessary
to the smooth functioning of the body politic. Religious people
make the best citizens. But it is not necessary to have an established church to get the benefits of religion in the civic arena.
Small churches, as voluntary societies, can accomplish quite automatically all that is claimed for an established church and without
the cumbersome operations of state power behind them.

   The Enlightenment rationalism of which Jefferson was a representative emphasized a belief in the sufficiency of human reason
applied to all aspects of life. Belief in God was part of the system,
but it was a God who had created the universe and set it to run according to immutable laws, both physical and moral. Man's part is

---

7. See A. E. Dick Howard, "Up Against the Wall: The Uneasy Separation of Church
and State," in *Church, State and Politics,* edited by Jaye B. Hensel (Washington, DC.:
The Roscoe Pound American Trial Lawyers Foundation, 1982), 5–39.

to discover these laws and to conduct his life accordingly. The essence of religion is morality. That is, living according to the eternal principles of right and wrong, principles which are discernible for the free operation of human reason. Jefferson held that this pure moral code of religion found its perfection of expression in the teachings of Jesus, teachings which were, however, unfortunately entangled in a web of irrelevant doctrine. Jefferson's attempt to free this teaching from its dogmatic shackles is well known. He created his own version of the *New Testament*, selecting those sayings of Jesus which he considered indubitably authentic.

Since the Enlightenment the West has witnessed the emergence of a set of views which help explain contemporary attitudes toward religion. Voltaire urged the eradication of Christianity from the world of higher culture, but he was willing to have it remain in the stables and in the scullery.[8] Mill repudiated Christianity, but not the religion of humanity which he thought to be, from the point of view of the state, a useful thing.[9] Comte, more benevolent in his attitude to Christian practice than either Voltaire or Mill and in spite of denial of all metaphysical validity to religious belief, was willing to accept as a civic good the moral and ritual traditions of at least Catholic Christianity.[10] Durkheim was not so positive. For him a major task of the state is to free individuals from partial societies, such as families, religious collectives, and labor and professional groups. Modern individualism, Durkheim agrees, depends on preventing the absorption of individuals into secondary or mediating groups. In antiquity, religious and political institutions were but parts of a whole social fabric, an organized social life to

8. *Voltaire's Notebooks*, edited by Theodore Testerman, 2 vols. (Genève: Institut et Musée, 1952), Vol. 2, 375 ff.

9. Voltaire, *Nature and Utility of Religion* (New York: The Liberal Arts Press, 1958).

10. "Plan of the Scientific Operations Necessary for Reorganizing Society," in *On Intellectuals*, edited by Philip Rieff (Garden City, NY: Doubleday, 1969).

which men could not but conform. It is, says Durkheim, only in modern circumstances, brought about by the centralization of government that individuals acquire personal freedom.[11]

It is in this context that the French philosopher Jacques Maritain (1882–1973) offered a contemporary statement of what may be regarded as the classical view of the relation between church and state. Although he was a Frenchman, his positions were formed largely in the American context. Junior colleagues such as Yves Simon and John Courtney Murray were influenced by him as they continued the discussion from a natural law viewpoint.

In a series of lectures he gave at the University of Chicago in 1949 and subsequently published as *Man and the State,* Maritain makes a number of distinctions which enable him to deal quickly with some of the issues raised in the above historical sketch. These distinctions are not original to Maritain, but they serve to organize some of the elements of the discussion. The most basic distinction is that between "community" and "society."[12] A community, as defined by Maritain, is a natural structure, having its basis in regional, ethnic, linguistic, or class affinities. Societies, on the other hand, are deliberately brought into being as their members organize to achieve agreed-upon ends. Examples of societies are structures such as business corporations, labor unions, and professional associations. In a community, in contrast to a society, social relations proceed from given historical situations and environments; collective patterns of feeling have the upper hand over personal consciousness, and the individual appears as the product of the social group. But in a society, personal consciousness and leadership are

11. *The Elementary Forms of Religious Life,* translated by J. W. Swain (New York: Collier, 1961), and *Moral Education* (New York: Macmillan, 1961).

12. Jacques Maritain, *Man and the State* (Chicago: University of Chicago Press, 1951), 2ff.

foremost. Societies are shaped by individuals. The family is notably one such society. Though it is the outcome of natural forces, it is fundamentally the product of personal decisions. A society, observes Maritain, always gives rise to communities and community feelings within or around itself. A community, however, is not likely to develop into a society, though it can be the natural soil from which some societal organization springs up through reason.

With this understanding of community and society Maritain can say the nation is a community, not a society. The nation is something ethico-social; it is a human community based on the fact of birth and lineage. "An ethnic community, generally speaking, can be defined as a community of patterns of feeling rooted in the physical soil of the origin of the group as well as in the moral soil of history; it becomes a nation when this factual situation enters the sphere of self-awareness."[13] When the ethnic group becomes conscious of the fact that it constitutes a community of patterns of feeling and possesses its own unity and individuality, its own will to endure its existence, then in some sense it becomes a nation. A nation is a community of people, usually with a common language, who have become aware of themselves as history has made them. Put another way, a nation is a community of people who treasure their own past and who love themselves as history has made them. The nation may be said to have a calling.

The nation is not to be confused with the body politic. Nor is the nation to be identified with the state. Maritain finds the notion of "national state" particularly abhorrent.[14] When a state attempts to impose national characteristics, it becomes totalitarian. National community gives rise to political society, but a plurality of national communities can exist within the same body politic. Pre-World War II Germany was a complex of nations which were

13. Ibid., 5.
14. Ibid., 7.

unable to bring about a genuine body politic. Germany made up for that frustration by an unnatural exaltation of national feeling and the unnatural nation-state. On the other hand, the Austro-Hungarian double crown created a state, but it was unable to produce a nation. France and the United States, says Maritain, have been able to produce a single nation centered on the body politic.

Both the body politic and the state are societies. Though the terms "body politic" and "state" are often used synonymously, they should be distinguished. They differ as whole to part. The body politic is the whole. The primary condition for the existence of the body politic is a common sense of justice, but friendship may be said to be its life-giving form. A civic outlook requires a sense of devotion and mutual love as well as a sense of justice and law. These attitudes of mind and will are carried primarily in heritage which itself is preserved by mediating or secondary institutions. Nothing matters more, in the order of material causality, to the life and preservation of the body politic than the accumulated energy and historical continuity of that national community which it has caused to exist. Common inherited experience and moral and intellectual instinct are its basis. Political life and the very existence and prosperity of the body politic depend on the vitality of family, economic, cultural, educational, and religious life.[15]

The state in Maritain's analysis is part of the body politic, that part concerned with the common welfare, the public order, and the administration of public affairs. The state is the part which specializes in the interest of the whole. It is not a man or a body of men but is rather a set of institutions combined into a unified machine. It is made up of experts or specialists in public order and welfare. It constitutes an embodiment of an impersonal, lasting superstructure. When functioning properly, it is rational and bound

15. Ibid., 11.

by law. As an instrument of the body politic the state is an agency entitled to use power and coercion. The state is the superior part of the body politic, but it is not superior to the body politic; it exists for man. The state is neither a whole, nor a person, nor the subject of a right. The common good of the political society is the final aim of the state and comes before the immediate aim of the state, which is the maintenance of the public order. The special temptation of the state is to exceed its mandate. Power tends to increase power. When it overreaches its mandate, the state tends to ascribe to itself a peculiar common good, namely, its own self-preservation and growth.

When the state mistakes itself for the whole of political society and takes upon itself the performance of tasks which normally pertain to the body politic or its organs, we have what Maritain calls the "paternalistic state." From the political point of view, the state is at its best when it is most restrained in seeking the common good. When it takes upon itself the organizing, controlling or managing of the economic, commercial, industrial, or cultural forms, it has transcended its skill and competence. If the state attempts to become a boss or a manager in business or industry, or a patron of art, or a leading spirit in the affairs of culture, science, or philosophy, it betrays its nature.[16]

The state receives its authority from the body politic, that is, the people. The people have a natural right to self-government. They exercise this right when they establish a constitution, written or unwritten. The people are the multitude of human persons who unite under just laws, by mutual friendship, for their common good. But the people not only constitute a body politic; as human persons they each have a spiritual soul and a super-temporal destiny. The people are above the state; the people are not for the state, but the state is for the people.

16. Ibid., 21

Maritain is at pains to emphasize the primacy of the spiritual. From the religious point of view, the common good of the body politic implies an intrinsic though indirect ordination to something which transcends it. In its own order the state is under the command of no superior authority, but the order of eternal life is superior in itself to the order of temporal life. The two orders need not create a conflict. From a secular perspective the church is an institution concerned with the spiritual in the life of the believer. "From the point of view of the common good, the activities of citizens as members of the church have an impact on the common good."[17] Thus the church in one sense is in the body politic, but in another and important sense, she transcends it.

The church and the body politic cannot live and develop in sheer isolation from and ignorance of one another. It is the same human person who is simultaneously a member of the body politic and a member of a church. An absolute division is both impossible and absurd. There must be cooperation. But what form should the cooperation take? It is evident that we no longer live in a sacral age. If classical antiquity or medieval Christianity were characterized by a unity of faith and if that unity of faith was required for a political unity, such does not now seem to be the case. Religious plurality is a fact, and the modern situation seems to demonstrate that religious unity is not a prerequisite for political unity. Neither can the church wield authority over the state nor call emperors, kings, princes, and even entire nations, to account. Indeed, the opposite is frequently the case, with the church seeking freedom within the political order to develop her own institutions.

The twentieth century has witnessed governments taking upon themselves more and more the role which Alexis de Tocqueville (1805–59) feared most, namely, that of an immense and tutelary power catering to all needs. In an age of limited government, be-

17. Ibid., 149–52.

fore government began to play a role in ordering a vast range of social and economic activities, the doctrine of "strict separation" or of "a benevolent neutrality" requiring that the government provide no aid of any kind to religion may have made some sense. On the other hand, an age of positive government, equating neutrality with a strict "no aid" position may be less tenable. As we have seen, the framers of the U.S. Constitution expected religion to play a part in the established social order and also assumed that the state would play a minimal role in forming that order. In our own time, the question of how to treat religious groups and interests has become a fundamentally different one. It can be argued that political equality for religious groups requires that they be able to participate in and have access to the benefits of government programs on the same basis as other groups.

In contrast to the confidence which Mill, Durkheim, and Dewey placed in the dynamism of a secular society, a number of contemporary thinkers have some reservations. It has been suggested that we are only now beginning to understand how intimately and profoundly the vitality of any society is bound up with its religion. Many have argued that the survival of Western culture demands unity as well as freedom. If men and women try to create a society in which there is no fundamental agreement about good and evil, they will fail; if, having based a society on common agreement and the agreement goes, the society will disintegrate.[18]

Robert Nisbet (1913–96) speaks of "the pre-democratic strata of values and institutions which alone make political freedom possible. . . . To lose, as I believe we are losing," says Nisbet, "the structure provided by inherited values is surely among the more desolating facts in the present decline of the West."[19] Christopher

18. Lord Patrick Devlin, *The Enforcement of Morals* (London: Oxford University Press, 1965), 11.
19. Robert Nisbet, *Twilight of Authority* (New York: Oxford University Press, 1979), 223.

Dawson (1898–1970) maintains that it is the religious impulse that supplies the cohesive force which unifies the society and the culture. The greatest civilizations of the world, Dawson suggests, do not produce the great religions as a kind of cultural by-product; in a very real sense, the greatest religions are the foundations on which the great civilizations rest."[20] And John Courtney Murray wrote, "Nothing more imperils both the common good of the earthly city and the supra-temporal interests of truth in human minds than a weakening and breaking down of the internal springs of conscience.[21] In judgments of this sort Maritain would indeed concur. Like Devlin, Nisbet, Dawson, and Murray, he would affirm that much is at stake.

Maritain leaves unresolved the problem of moral unity in a people. He cannot opt for the "common faith," described by John Dewey, a naturalistic credo that goes beyond the merely political. Instead, he is tempted by the "civic faith" delineated by his friend John Courtney Murray in *We Hold These Truths*. But how are the wellsprings of conscience and civic faith to be maintained? Before his death Maritain was to see the breakdown of inherited morality on all fronts. A common Christian outlook with respect to matters such as civic decorum, contraception, divorce, abortion, homosexuality, pornography, and capital punishment gave way. The morality commonly affirmed in the nineteenth century came to be denied by great numbers. The denial has been translated into law, if not by legislation then by the courts as they have interpreted the law.

Maritain recognizes that if religious institutions are to possess any authority, it will be the result of moral influence, the result of their being able through their teachings to reach the human con-

20. Christopher Dawson, *Religion and the Rise of Western Culture* (New York: Sheed and Ward, 1950), Chap. 1.

21. John Courtney Murray, *We Hold These Truths* (New York: Sheed and Ward, 1960), 161.

science. Of course, this way of carrying spiritual primacy can be checked by an opposite course of action, chosen by other citizens. But Maritain believes that a free exchange of ideas, despite possible setbacks, is a surer way of attaining influence in the long run. The church is less likely to lose her independence, for if the state is enlisted to implement ecclesiastical goals, the state is likely to serve its own purposes first. History has taught us that the secular arm is always eager to exercise control, to take the initiative.

Maritain assumes that the church is free to educate and that she is positioned to compete as an equal in the marketplace of ideas. He is conscious that such may not be the actual case, even in the United States, which he more or less takes as a paradigm. The issue is not clear-cut. On the one hand, Maritain affirms, "Freedom of inquiry, even at the risk of error, is the normal condition for men to access to truth, so that freedom to search for God in their own way, for those who have been brought up in ignorance or semi-ignorance of Him, is the normal condition in which to listen to the message of the Gospel."[22] Yet he is convinced, "Willingly or unwillingly States will be obliged to make a choice for or against the Gospel. They will be shaped either by the totalitarian spirit or by the Christian spirit."[23] The West, symbolically at least, continues in many ways to reflect its Christian heritage. Maritain believes that the public acknowledgment of God's existence is good and should be maintained. It is to be expected that a public expression of common faith will assume the form of that Christian confession to which history and the traditions of the West are most vitally linked. As for the citizens who are unbelievers, they will have only to realize that the body politic as a whole is just as free with regard to the public expression of its own faith as they, as individuals, are

22. Maritain, *Man and the State*, 162.
23. Ibid., 159.

free with regard to the private expression of their own non-religious conviction.[24]

In discussing the beneficent influence of religion, Maritain does not confuse morality and religion. The essence of religion for Maritain is, as it was for Augustine and Aquinas, primarily worship. Worship is a species of justice, the paying of a debt to God. Furthermore, morality does not conceptually depend on religion. Moral norms have a life of their own, independent of religion. This is not to say that the religious mind is confined to the endorsement of secular morality. Morality is in many respects changed within a theistic context. Obligations toward God as well as men are recognized. Within Christianity, in particular, suffering and death take on a meaning which they do not have within a secular context. An ascetic life of renunciation, or one of sacrifice, acquires a value which it would not have within a purely materialistic order. A conception of God as personal and loving has implications; only then do prayer and contemplation become habits of mind to be recommended. In the face of adversity, a religious outlook can inspire hope, holding out a promise of eternal reward for actions that bear no temporal fruit. Christianity counsels patience, love, understanding, long-suffering, and humility. Some, but not all of these, conflict with a purely secular outlook.[25]

Other contributions with which Maritain credits religion may be noted. One of the most important is the very one which Durkheim feared. The church, even in a religiously plural society, can stand between the government and the individual, providing a buffer between the two. Religious organizations perform this function by serving the individual in need, preventing him from becoming completely dependent upon the state for every material

24. Ibid., 172–73.
25. Ibid., 176ff.

necessity. In education and in the care of the sick, the orphaned, and the elderly, the religious institution can provide a type of help that respects the dignity of the person and which responds to individual requirements in a way that often eludes the best intentioned state institution.[26]

Other subtle but important side effects of a religious outlook include an historical sense and, if you will, a metaphysical sense. Through his religion, the believer is led to identify not simply with a present community of believers but with a community that has a history, a community that, in some cases, is thought to have been the recipient of a divine revelation. A religious people have a history, and the informed religious mind will attempt to capture that history in order to understand the forces which have shaped the message to which he is heir. The Jew, the Christian, and the Moslem all believe that they are in some sense God's chosen, that something has been revealed to them that has been denied to others. That revelation took place in time. In recapturing that time, the believer transcends his own period. Since sacral history is bound up with secular history, it is more than religious history that will command his attention.[27]

As to the metaphysical sense, the religious mind finds it impossible to discuss the content of its belief without invoking the categories of being. Jerusalem must borrow from Athens. The religious mind also has a sense for order. Nature is regarded as intelligible because it is the handiwork of the divine. It is not by accident that the modern university was born in a religious setting where there was the dual confidence in being's intelligibility and in man's ability to know, attended by further conviction that nature was there to

26. Ibid., 178–79.

27. Maritain expands this notion in a chapter entitled "Evangelical Inspiration and the Secular Conscience," in *Christianity and Democracy*, (London: Geoffrey Bles, 1945), 27ff.

be used for the benefit of man. These were no mean insights and were to play major roles in the development of Western science and technology.[28]

Certain iconoclasts notwithstanding, religion also carries with it an appreciation for symbol. Religious ritual is one obvious form, employing a multiplicity of symbols. Religious literature is full of metaphor. Because of the ineffable character of that of which religion must speak, simile, allegory, and parables are second nature. The tendency to relate all things to God, to sanctify human acts and occasions, has created not only some of the most delightful feasts of the year, but some of the greatest painting and music and literature the world has known.[29]

Furthermore, it makes a difference whether things are referred to God or not. As many have seen, in a secular society the citizen's rights can only be the social compact of this society. But if rights are looked upon as God-given, if the state itself is accountable to a divine order of things, if civil law is not final, the quality of society can be quite different. The "divine right of kings" doctrine, so happily seized by Western monarchs, was in fact recognized as a Christian heresy. No medieval Christian king could subscribe to the notion that law came from him. Rather, the church taught that he should recognize that his will was subordinated to divine law and that his acts would be judged against a standard not of his making. The notion of God-given rights was taken for granted in the early days of our republic.

Finally, religion forces man to ask important questions, questions such as: What is the purpose of life? What is man's ultimate

---

28. *The Person and the Common Good* (London: Geoffrey Bles, 1948), 58. There is a passage in which Maritain speaks of the common good of intellects, "the intelligible treasure of culture in which minds communicate with one another." "It is better," he says, "to have Plato, Aristotle, Kant and St. Thomas, than to have St. Thomas alone."

29. See Maritain, "On Artistic Judgment," in *The Range of Reason*, 19ff.

destiny? What goods are indispensable? How should man behave toward himself, toward his neighbor, toward other peoples, toward nature? What should he consecrate? In raising these questions, religion stimulates a debate which is fruitful, even by its own light, even when it produces a Voltaire. As DeGaulle said of the atheist John Paul Sartre vis-à-vis the latter's contribution to France, "Sartre, he too serves."

RELIGION AND THE STATE UNDER U.S. CONSTITUTION

John Courtney Murray

Maritain's contribution to the discussion is an analysis which shows religion's indispensable function in society and the concomitant obligation of the state to provide an impartial and unencumbered aid to ensure enlightened internal development within religious bodies. This development alone makes possible a superior cultural contribution. John Courtney Murray (1904–67) was to carry Maritain's analysis one step further. Although focusing primarily on the situation in the United States, his observations transcend time and place. Like John Adams two centuries before, he wished to find those truths which all Americans presumably shared by virtue of citizenship. The basic problem, he was convinced, was not one of the relation of church to state but of the intellectual unity required for a nation to act.

For Murray, democracy is an effective mode of government. The democratic charter is not to be made an object of faith. The U.S. Constitution and the articles of its First Amendment are articles of peace, not part of a secular credo which renounces a role for religion in civic affairs. "If history makes one thing clear, it is that these clauses were the twin children of social necessity, the necessity of creating a social environment, protected by law, in which men of different faiths might live together in peace.[1] The American solution to the relationship between church and state was purely political. Among the various churches vying for allegiance none was to be preferred for the nation as a whole. Although in the beginning of the American republic nine states had established churches, eventually this principle was to be applied to the states as well. The result was political unity and stability without uniformity of religious belief and practice. The Gallic, "One law, one faith, one king," had been replaced by "political unity in the midst of religious plurality." But, Murray reasons, it does not follow from this that political unity can long endure in the absence of a moral consensus. "Nor has experience yet shown how, if at all, this moral consensus can survive amid all the ruptures of religious division, whose tendency is inherently disintegrative of all consensus and community."[2]

In 1960 Murray could write, "In America we have been rescued from the disaster of ideological parties."[3] Where such parties exist, the struggle for office becomes a struggle for power by which the opposing ideology may be destroyed. In contrast to certain Latin countries, the American experience of political unity has been striking, and to this the First Amendment has made a unique contribution. Murray is convinced that the Catholic church has profited from the American arrangement. In Latin countries, the church has alternately experienced privilege and persecution. Where it is thought that the business of government is the fostering of the commonwealth as ascertained by the church, the for-

1. John Courtney Murray, *We Hold These Truths* (New York: Sheed and Ward, 1960), 57.
2. Ibid., 73.
3. Ibid.

tunes of the church wax and wane with the transfer of political power. "In contrast, American government has not undertaken to represent transcendental truth in any of the versions of it current in American society."[4] It has not allied itself with one faith over another, but it has represented a core of commonly shared moral values. In a religiously plural society, government must be neutral in the face of religious claims; it cannot set itself up as a judge of religious truth. But pluralism itself creates certain problems: how much pluralism and what kinds of pluralism can a pluralist society stand?

The nature of the "public philosophy" is the issue which brought commentators from diverse viewpoints, Jewish, Protestant, and agnostic, into the same forum. Murray raised the question in this manner:

Is there a consensus generated by a common allegiance to the U.S. Constitution whereby the people acquire an identity, a collective sense of purpose, sufficient to serve as the basis for action? . . . Can we or can we not . . . achieve a successful conduct of our national affairs, foreign and domestic, in the absence of a consensus that will set our purposes, furnish a standard of judgment on policies; and establish the proper conditions for political dialogue?[5]

In Murray's judgment the civic consensus is constructed neither by psychological rationalizations nor by economic interest nor by purely pragmatic working hypotheses. "It is an ensemble of substantive truths, a structure of basic knowledge, an order of elementary affirmations that reflect realities inherent in the order of existence."[6] But he recognized that any systematic formulation of these truths is apt to meet resistance.

If there was once an American consensus, if the Founding Fa-

4. Ibid., 74.   5. *Time*, art. cit.
6. Murray, *We Hold These Truths*, 9.

thers knew what they meant by liberty, law, and by God, that consensus does not exist today.

The ethic which launched Western constitutionalism and endured long enough as a popular heritage to give essential form to the American system of government has now ceased to sustain the structure and direct the action of this constitutional commonwealth.[7]

Murray was convinced that the grounds for such a consensus still exist, at least ideally, in the natural law philosophy of Aristotle, the Stoics, and Aquinas. It is that tradition, reflected in the writings of Richard Hooker, John Locke, and others, which provided the principles on which the nation was founded. It is a philosophical tradition which surmounts religious difference, an intellectual tradition that is confident that the order of nature can be discerned and that what is good for man can be established.

For Murray, political life aims at a common good which is superior to a mere collection of individual goods. The fruit of common effort must, of course, flow back to the individual. But he was disturbed by the question: in the absence of a common way of looking at things, can there be an ascertainable common good? Murray's answer contrasts sharply with that entertained by contemporaries such as John Dewey and Sidney Hook (1902–89), who subscribed to an essentially Hobbesian account of the social order. From the point of view of Hobbes, society is not one entity but a collection of action groups, each pressing for advantage. According to Hobbes the source of government is the consent of those governed, taken one by one. The individual is the sole source of the right or the good and as an autonomous agent is subject neither to given norms nor to a naturally determined end. Hobbes makes no attempt to subordinate the individual act of self-aggrandizement to the public good. Self-interest, he holds, is not only the dominant

7. Ibid.

motive in politics, but enlightened self-interest is the proper remedy for social ills. Men, he believes, are constituted differently in temperament, biography, and intelligence, and consequently identify the good for themselves in radically different ways. Self-interest is not to be taken as evidence of moral defect but as evidence of disparate personality.

In Murray's judgment, when one acknowledges a common good, separate from and superior to the private goods of individual men, the function of government becomes that of conflict management. Given the fact that litigious subjects are likely to press for special privileges and exemptions for themselves, bargaining and negotiating are natural features of public life. Under such conditions the sovereign is not the representative of the common will; he is the common object of separate wills. In the exercise of his authority, the sovereign is restrained only by the diverse purposes of his subjects. The sovereign assists his subjects in the pursuit of happiness not by defining the goals which the members of society ought collectively to pursue, but by removing obstacles to happiness, which is privately defined. Public order thus has its sources in negotiations between individually situated political actors. Such a view in Murray's judgment can only lead to disaster. In both theory and practice, those who defend special interests do not acknowledge any need to attend to the perceptions or reactions of others who do not share their view. Rights are pushed no matter what the consequences. A compliant or weak judiciary is apt to rule in favor of an individual claimant against the common good.

Murray addresses the basic but difficult question: In the absence of a common way of looking at things, can the notion of the common good play a role in thinking about the ends of government? Is it necessary that a philosophy, such as that which supports the notion of a common good, prevail in order to exercise a beneficial influence in the social setting? Is it not sufficient that it keep alive and defend its vantage point? May not calls to attend to the common good have their effect on policy even if the philosophy underlying the concept is imperfectly understood or flatly rejected? Murray's answer is that a working consensus need not embrace all sectors of the society and that it need not embrace equally those which do not share it. The existence of intellectual conflict, suggests Murray, is not evidence that there cannot be agreement on very important matters. The acceptance of principles such as the rule of law, the separation of powers, the freedom of belief, the freedom of association, and the representation of beliefs and interest do not depend on metaphysical agreement, although these principles obviously need a defense. The danger of course is that in the absence of a set of commonly acknowledged principles special interest groups may prevail. Irving Babbit saw this when he wrote in *Democracy and Leadership,* "No movement illustrates more clearly than the supposedly democratic movement the way in which the will of highly organized and resolute minorities may prevail over the will of the inert and unorganized mass."[8]

Murray, in attempting to articulate the truths undergirding U.S. Constitutional government, draws a list that is surprisingly long. On his account, we can readily identify the broad purposes of the nation, or, if you will, the aims of government. With respect to means, standards of judgment may vary and there will be policy differences. But we can speak about these things because there is a basis of communication, a universe of discourse. Speaking of his fellow citizens, Murray writes, "We hold in common a concept of the nature of law and its relationship to reason and to will, to social fact and to political purpose. We understand the complex relationship between law and freedom."[9] As a people we have in common

8. Irving Babbit, *Democracy and Leadership* (New York: Houghton Mifflin, 1924), 290–91.

9. Murray, *We Hold These Truths,* 81.

an idea of justice, we believe in the principle of consent, we distinguish between law and morality, and we understand the relationship between law and freedom. We also recognize criteria for good law, that is, norms of jurisprudence. As a people we "grasp the notion of law as a force for orderly change as well as social stability."[10] Most law is rooted in the shared idea of the personal dignity or sacredness of man, *res sacra homo*. This sacredness guarantees him certain immunities and endows him with certain empowerments generally recognized.

Neither ideally nor in the United States, need consensus prevent dissent. In the United States the dissenters are not placed beyond the pale of social or civil rights. Those who refuse to subscribe often come from the ranks of the literati and have the media at their disposal. They are not only the academicians, the professional students of philosophy, politics, economics, and history, but also the politicians, writers, journalists, and clergy. Murray calls them "clerks." Oxford professor John Gray speaks of them as "the intellectuals" and is wary of them because of their nonconformist tendencies.[11] They lack the same stake in society as those have who are responsible for its industrial and economic success, and possibly for family and community tranquility. They are apt to be disruptive in any scenario.

Murray carries the question from domestic to international consideration. "Can we or can we not achieve a successful conduct of our affairs, foreign and domestic, in the absence of a consensus that will set our purpose, furnish a standard of judgment on policies, and establish the proper condition for political dialogue?"[12]

10. Ibid.

11. John Gray, "Society and Intellectuals: The Persistence of Estrangement and Wishful Thinking," in *The Many Faces of Socialism* (New Brunswick, NJ: Transaction Books, 1987).

12. Murray, *We Hold These Truths*, 86.

The absence of a public philosophy, Murray thought, is never more evident than in discussions concerning the structure, content, and orientation of military policies. In the United States, he says we have not articulated, for example, the political and moral ends for which we are prepared to use force. Murray cites the former national security advisor Henry Kissinger, who wrote in *Nuclear Weapons and Foreign Policy*[13] "It is not true that America can intelligently construct and morally put to use a defense establishment in the absence of a public philosophy concerning the use of force as a moral and political act."[14] Until we can articulate an American consensus with regard to our truths, our purposes, and our values, unless we can agree on fundamentals, public policy will continue to be projected out of a vacuum in the governmental mind into a vacuum in the popular mind."[15] The only bright spot, Murray suggests, is Kissinger judgment that in the absence of intellectual agreement, our instinctive wisdom permits us to cope and survive. Murray's observations could be applied equally to France, Germany, and beyond.

Murray is careful to note that consensus does not mean majority opinion. "Public opinion is a shorthand phrase expressing the fact that a large body of the community has reached or may reach specific conclusions in some particular situation. Those conclusions are spontaneously, perhaps emotionally reached usually from some unstated but very real premises. The 'public consensus' is the body of these general unstated premises which come to be accepted. It furnishes the basis for public opinion."[16] The consensus is a doctrine or a judgment that commands public agreement on its merits. "The consensus is not in any sense an ideology; its

13. Henry Kissinger, "The Need for Doctrine" (New York: Harper and Brothers, 1957), as cited by Murray in *We Hold These Truths*, 91.

14. Murray, *We Hold These Truths*, 95.   15. Ibid., 102–3.

16. Ibid., 106.

close relation to concrete experience rescues it from that fate."[17] The public consensus is a moral conception. "Only the theory of natural law is able to give an account of the public moral experience that is the public consensus. The consensus itself is simply the tradition of reason as emergent in developing form in the special circumstances of . . . political-economic life."[18]

Murray is aware that the doctrine of natural law is associated with Catholicism. But he is quick to point out that the doctrine has no Catholic presuppositions. Its presuppositions are threefold: "that man is intelligent; that reality is intelligible; and that reality as grasped by intelligence imposes on the will an obligation that it be obeyed in its demands for action or abstention."[19] The assumption is that rational human nature works competently in most men, although intellectual judgment alone is not enough. Not only knowledge but rectitude of judgment is required.

"Natural law theory does not pretend to do more than it can, which is to give a philosophical account of the moral experience of humanity and to lay down a charter of essential humanism."[20] It does not show the individual the way to sainthood, but only to temporal fulfillment. "It does not promise to transform society in to the city of God on earth, but only to prescribe, for the purposes of law and social custom, the minimum of morality which must be observed by the member of society, if the social environment is to be human and habitable."[21] To inquire what natural law is, means to inquire, on the one hand, what the human mind is and what it can know, and on the other hand, what human society is and to what ends it should work. Its hallmark is its empirical character, its fidelity to evidence derived from common experience and the sciences.

17. Ibid., 109.　　　　　　18. Ibid.
19. Ibid., 297.　　　　　　20. Ibid.
21. As quoted by the *New York Times*, October 10, 1963.

For John Dewey, whom we previously considered, there can be only one society, one law, one power, and one faith, namely, a civic faith that is the unifying bond of the community. Dewey would banish from the political sphere the divisive force of religion. His view has been forcefully represented by disciples such as Sidney Hook, who for one has no quarrel with religion taken as a purely private matter. What alarms him is religion in an institutional form, visible, corporate, and organized, a community of thought that presumes to sit superior to and in judgment on the community of democratic thought. Hook thinks that religion possessed of social structures by means of which it can voice its judgments and perhaps cause them to prevail is at variance with a secular concept of civic life. From a purely secular perspective, civil society is the highest societal form of human life. Civil law is the highest form of law and is not subject to judgment by pure ethical canons. Thus, while recognizing its legality, Hook would decry the existence of the parochial (religious) school system as "educationally and democratically unsound" because it separates a large segment of our youth and imbues them with quite a divergent outlook.[22] For Hook there is no eternal order of truth and justice; there are no universal verities which command assent, no universal moral law which requires obedience. The ultimate values espoused by society do not flow from the recognition of some antecedently derived notion of the common good. Rather, ultimate value is to be identified with the democratic process itself. The democratic faith is belief in the efficacy of the process.

Murray's natural law philosophy and Dewey's pragmatic naturalism lead to many of the same conclusions in the practical order, and both recognized this. Their differences are metaphysical and epistemological and illustrate the difference between a Dewey-type

22. "Dr. Hook Criticizes Parochial Schools," Associated Press Dispatch, October 10, 1963.

instrumentalism and a classical natural law outlook. For Murray there exists a body of truths about human nature and about that which is required for human fulfillment which can be passed from generation to generation. Thus the ancients, no less intelligent or observant than we, are thought to speak to us across the ages about an essentially unchanging human nature, and, for Murray, it behooves us to return to those authors whose works have been appreciated and commented upon for centuries. That body of truths rests on a set of metaphysical assumptions, viz., that there is such a thing as human nature and that certain ends can be identified as proper to it and others as inappropriate. Thus one can say that a life of the mind, being proper to man as rational animal, is preferable to a "simple sense life" that the laws of the state should promote those structures and activities that contribute to self-fulfillment; that self-fulfillment cannot take place apart from community; and that the state, is obligated to defend the family and the rights of private property, and to ensure access to a basic education for all of its citizens. Those commonly accepted truths serve as principles in the prudential order. The prudential judgment itself does not share in the certitude characteristic of the universal or time-transcending principle. The prudential judgment is made in context; its value is determined not solely by principle but by the empirical data available. Concrete options may even foster a reexamination of abstract principles. Thus, the further removed from the basic truths regarding human nature and society, the more precarious the judgment. For example, "respect for one's parents" taken as a principle does not dictate a specific manner of caring for an aging parent. Circumstances direct prudential decision.

The pragmatist's preference of solving each problem in the context in which it arises does not abrogate for him an appeal to principle. He too will invoke principle, but he is not willing to weave those principles into a consistent whole or anchor them in a particular conception of human nature or conception of human fulfillment. Thus contradictory principles may be invoked in different contexts without inconsistency. If a principle itself is challenged, it too is defended in the context at hand without recourse to a set of constants. For this reason the pragmatist is often considered to be sophistical in argument. The metaphysics to which he is committed often goes unstated and is placed beyond direct confrontation.

The pragmatic naturalism of Dewey's variety, although it eschews metaphysics, is nevertheless a materialism which denies evidence of the existence of God and therefore the need for religion in the lives of the people. The beauty attendant the temple, ritual, and feast is held to be built on chimerical foundations. Man is regarded as through and through physicochemical, having his origin, growth, and decay in nature. This has implications for ethics since there is no transcendent end for human life, which in turn has implications for the role of the state. The most noble aspiration one can have is to make this a better place for future generations. Hence the emphasis on training for service and power. Unlike Murray's, Dewey's educational philosophy, with its assumption of "progress," its insistence on personal experience, and its orientation to an idealized future, tends to denigrate the inherited and even the study of history. Classical languages are not required to gain access to what is considered an irrelevant antiquity. Since, according to Dewey, one of the primary aims of education is that of challenging the inherited, education does not consist in appropriation of the literature that has nourished the West since classical Greece.

Murray could speak of this as a new barbarism threatening the life of reason embodied in law and custom. The perennial work of the barbarian is to undermine rational standards of judgment, to corrupt inherited wisdom by which the people have always lived, and to do this not by spreading new beliefs but by creating a climate of doubt and bewilderment in which clarity about the larger aims of life is dimmed and the self-confidence of the people destroyed.[23]

Murray in his day was not optimistic that the West could in the near future recover its patrimony.

The Spanish-born, Harvard University professor George Santayana, writing in 1913 for an American audience, observed:

The present age is a critical one and interesting to live in. The civilisation characteristic of Christendom has not disappeared, yet another civilisation has begun to take its place. We still understand the value of religious faith. . . . On the other hand the shell of Christendom is broken. The unconquerable mind of the East, the pagan past, the industrial socialistic future confront it with their equal authority. Our whole life and mind is saturated with the slow upward filtration of a new spirit—that of an emancipated, atheistic, international democracy.[24]

Obviously it does make a difference to society whether people believe in and worship God. Society does have a stake in the presence or absence of religion. Although morality and religion are not to be identified, it is evident that religion carries with it a code of values. Both Maritain and Murray affirm that for the sake of virtue in the citizenry, is it incumbent on the state to encourage religious instruction and practice. As we have seen, throughout the centuries that judgment has been sustained by many regimes for good or evil. It was left to the United States to show in its First Amendment to the Constitution, "Congress shall make no law respecting an establishment of religion or prohibit the free exercise thereof."

23. Murray, *We Hold These Truths*, 13.
24. George Santayana, "Winds of Doctrine," in *The Works of George Santayana* (New York: Charles Scribner's Sons, 1937), 3.

Yet that balance which has served the nation well has been subverted by an activist judiciary pursuing a purely secular agenda, reflecting the agnosticism of the academy. Murray did not live to witness the fulfillment of his prediction. The logic of irreligion has been played out with consequences for society.

ORIENTAL RELIGIONS AND SIMILAR
CULTURAL MANIFESTATIONS

Buddhism, Confucianism

The theories of religion heretofore considered subsequent to the classical period have focused on Christianity. While Christianity shaped Western culture and in fact may be said to define Western identity, a full treatment of religion from an historical or sociological perspective would have to consider the religions of the Middle East and the Far East as well as manifestations of religion in a primitive stage. The word "religion" as commonly employed is rather elastic, and it is difficult to define it in such a way that it will suit all scholars and be adequately applicable to all the phenomena which are sometimes labeled religious.

In approaching Eastern "religion," it must be kept in mind that ethics of itself is not a religion. This is clear from the work of the Greek philosophers and from the sayings of Confucius. The ethics of Aristotle is in no way a religious exercise. He did not derive his code of morality from anything but an analysis of human nature, one made without reference to God or something beyond death. Ethics, specifically the virtue of justice, may dictate worship, but this puts ethics outside of religion and in a way over religion. It is evident that personal morality is quite possible without religious commitment, as seen from the worthy behavior of many self-styled atheists. If the morally good man need not be religious, conversely a man who professes a religion may not be moral.

There is another point to remember. Socially conducted ritual, symbolic and formal, need not be religious to touch the core of one's beliefs and feelings. Many patriotic rituals are definitely not religious, such as flag ceremonies where heads are bared and dedications made. The Japanese understood the worship of their emperor as an act of patriotism and not a religious act of worship. During the French Revolution the Robespierrian cult of reason was militantly antireligious although it fostered ritual and cult which mimicked that of Christianity. Similarly, the belief in invisible powers is not necessarily religious. In magic and animism the universe is conceived of visible and invisible agents. These agents are not gods but component elements of the world, not differing essentially from the grosser material elements which surround man.

No one will deny that Christian groups are religious or that Judaism is a religion. Similarly the Islamic faith is definitely a religious phenomenon. So too is Shinto. But is Buddhism a religion or merely a form of asceticism involving a theory of reincarnation? Is Brahmanism a religion or only a culture based on a philosophy which can be called religious? Many would consider Buddhism and Brahmanism to be religions, but Brahmanism is at its core pantheistic, just as Buddha's doctrine is atheistic. Confucianism must be recognized as a moral philosophy that has performed for China and those nations influenced by China the functions which Christianity has performed in the West. In Confucianism we find a natural wisdom, a sense of propriety, and a ritual which reflects that wisdom. In the West we find its analogue in the manners of the well bred. From the second century B.C. to the Communist takeover in the twentieth, Confucianism has been synonymous with learning in China.

Confucius (551–479 B.C.) is the Latinized name of *Kung-futzu*, *Kung* being his surname and *futzu* the name for master. Confucius, it may be noted, is a near contemporary of Socrates (c. 470–399 B.C.). Early as a youth Confucius established himself as a master of ritual. The original word for ritual is *li*, which means a sense of propriety, the order of things. Some translate it as the "moral and religious institutions of the Three Dynasties." In fact, Confucianism has been known in China through the centuries as *li chiao*, the religion of *li*, or "ritual." This conception of *li*, meaning much more than mere ritualism in the Western sense, is Confucius's central theme for an ideal social order. Throughout his life, he sought to restore a social order based on love for one's kind and respect for authority, of which the social rites of public worship and other festivities employing ritual and music are to be the outward symbols.

Confucius attributed the ills of his day to the fact that the leaders of society had neglected the old rites or were performing them incorrectly, or were usurping rites and ceremonies to which they were not entitled. He believed that the neglect and abuse of the rites reflected a deepening moral chaos and the beginning of spiritual darkness. In his judgment, such was the state of affairs in his day throughout China.

Before Confucius's time, education was a privilege of the aristocracy. Confucius sought to change that. Advocating the position that "where education took root, class distinction would not exist," he was the first person to bring the knowledge previously reserved for the temples of a ruling class to the marketplaces of the common man. Over a period of forty years, he taught 3,000 pupils, of whom seventy-two had mastered the "six arts"—ritual, music, archery, driving of chariot, history, and mathematics. His students came from all parts of China, not just the state of Lu, but from Wei, Chi, Chin, Cheng, Tsin, Sung, Wu, and Wueh. His teaching was unheard of before him, and his popularization of learning produced the unexpected effect of cultural unity for China, coming some three hundred years before Chin Shih Hunag was responsible for the political unification of the country in the first Chinese empire.

For use in teaching, Confucius edited the so-called Six Classics:

1. *Shih Ching (Book of Odes)*, a collection of 305 songs and sacred anthems, said to be chosen from more than 3,000.

2. *Li Chi (Book of Rites)*, allegedly a record of government systems and rituals of the early Chou dynasty.

3. *Shu Ching (Book of History)*, composed of early historic documents, chiefly King's proclamations, the earliest of Chinese documents and the most archaic in style of all classics.

4. *Chun Chiu (Annals of Spring and Autumn)*, written by Confucius, a chronicle of events from 722 to 481 B.C., based on the history of the state of Lu; the only work attributed to him.

5. *I Ching (Book of Changes)*, the philosophy of mutations in human events, originally a divination system based on changing arrangements of the lines of an octogram but which developed into a full philosophy for human conduct in varying circumstances.

6. *Yueh Ching (Book of Music)*, a book which has been completely lost.

With the *Book of Music* no longer existing, the Six Classics are now only five.[1]

After Confucius's death, two chapters were taken from the *Book*

---

1. See Anna Wing-tsit Chau, *Encyclopedia Britanica* 15th ed. (1974) Vol. 4, 1104–1108, for an authoritative and succinct discussion of the classical Confucian texts.

of Rites and became two independent books: *Ta Hsueh (The Great Learning)* and *Chung Yung (The Golden Mean)*. But the most popular of all was *Lun Yu (Analects of Confucius)*, a collection of the master's sayings recorded by his disciples. A century later, Confucianism found its most effective spokesman in Mencius (372–289 B.C.), who since has been regarded by the Chinese as their "second sage." His disciples collected his sayings into a book bearing his name. Together these volumes form the treasure of Confucian teachings as well as classical Chinese learnings and are known as the *Four Books* and *Five Classics.*

Central to Confucius's teaching is his identification of politics with ethics. His definition of "ritual and music" embodied the entire aim of the Confucian social order. His intention was to create a moral basis for peace in society, out of which political peace would naturally ensue. His idea of government was:

if the state guides the people by governmental measures and regulates them by the threat of punishment, the people will try to keep out of jail but will have no sense of honor or shame. But guide the people by virtue and regulate them by *li* (sense of propriety), and the people will have a sense of honor and respect.[2]

A detailed study of Confucianism would disclose that it is more a humanism than a religion. The measure of man is man. The central tenet of Confucian teaching is *jen:* humanity, benevolence, perfect virtue, or "the moral sense," which is probably closest to it. The other tenet is *shu:* tolerance or reciprocity. Confucius repeatedly said: "Do not do unto others what you would not have others do unto you." In explaining *jen,* Confucius listed five virtues: "Courtesy, magnanimity, good faith, diligence, and kindness. He who is courteous is not humiliated, he who is magnanimous wins the

2. *The Analects of Confucius,* translated by David H. L. (Bethesda, MD: Premier Publishing Co., 1999), 2.3.

multitude, he who is of good faith is trusted by the people, he who is diligent attains his objective, and he who is kind can get service from the people."[3] On another occasion, when asked about the meaning of *jen,* he replied in two words: "Love men."[4]

Since in the West much of this moral teaching is associated with the teachings of Christ and with Christianity, it is natural that Confucianism is often thought of as a religion. With respect to the social and political implications of his basic insights, Confucius stressed personal moral cultivation as the basis of a world order. *Hsiao,* or filial piety, is the basis of all order.[5] For having acquired the habits of love and respect in the home, one cannot but extend this mental attitude of love and respect to other people's parents and elder brothers and to the authorities of the state. The idea is best expressed by the opening chapter of *Ta Hsueh (The Great Learning):*

The ancients who wished to preserve the fresh or clear character of the people of the world would first set about ordering their national life. Those who wished to order their national life would first set about regulating their family life. Those who wished to regulate their family life would first set about cultivating their personal life. Those who wished to cultivate their personal life would first set about setting their hearts right. Those who wished to set their hearts right would first set about making their wills sincere.[6]

Confucius's ideal man is the *chun tzu,* or gentleman. He is not an aristocrat but merely kind, a gentleman with moral principles. He is a man who loves learning, who is calm himself and perfectly at ease and constantly careful of his own conduct, believing that by example he has great influence over society in general. He is also perfectly at ease in his own station of life and has a certain contempt for the mere luxuries of living. Confucius said: "The gentle-

---

3. Ibid., 17.6.
5. Ibid., 1.2.

4. Ibid., 12.22a.
6. Ibid., 17.8.

man makes demands on himself; the inferior man makes demands on others."[7]

These ideas of Confucius have dictated the development of Chinese history for the past twenty-five centuries until Mao Zedong's cultural revolution. They not only exerted a vital influence on the Chinese way of life but also on those of Korea, Japan, the Ryukyus, and Vietnam. For eight hundred years the Confucian classics were the basic text in Chinese education, known to every school-age boy and girl. As a political system aiming at the restoration of a feudal order, Confucianism may be long out of date, but as a system of humanist culture, as a fundamental viewpoint concerning the conduct of life and of society, and above all, as a way of life which has proved its value after 2,500 years, there is no doubt that it is still very much alive and dear to the heart of those who cherish their Chinese heritage.

Buddhism as an intellectual and moral force has similarly shaped the culture of India and much of southeast Asia. Originating in India in the fifth century B.C., it owes its origin to the Buddha, Siddhartha Gautama, (f. 563 B.C.), a prince of the Shakya tribe of the Ganges states. With Confucianism it has to be considered one of the great Eastern moral systems undergirding a culture with its own peculiar art, architecture, sculpture, and literature. The term "buddha," literally meaning "enlightened one," is not a proper name but rather a title. The word is usually accompanied by an article, such as "the Buddha" or "a Buddha." Usually "The Buddha" unless otherwise indicated refers to Gautama the Buddha.

The teachings attributed to Buddha were transmitted orally by his disciples.[8] Some of his teaching is not unlike that of near West-

---

7. Ibid., 15.21.

8. This account relies heavily on Giuseppe Tucci, "Buddhism" in *Encyclopedia Britannica* (Chicago: 1974), Vol. 15, 374–403, and Joseph M. Kitagawa "History of Bud-

ern contemporaries, i.e., Thales of Miletus (f. 580 B.C.) And Heraclitus of Ephesus (540–480 B.C.). Readers of the pre-Socratics will recognize a common dictum. For example, all is impermanent, a flowing reality, whether of external things or the body-mind totality of the human individual. With these assertions, Gautama departed from traditional Indian thought in denying an essence or nature to things. A "self" or "soul" does not exist; there is nothing within us that is metaphysically real. There is no eternal "I," yet human beings are caught in the cycle of births and deaths because the extinction of life does not mean the end of existence but a projection to a new existence.

For this to happen, there must be an understanding of the mechanism by which man's psychophysical being evolves; otherwise one would remain indefinitely in the cycle of transitory existence. Certain laws must be acknowledged as true, e.g., the law of dependent origination, that is, the law that one condition arises out of another, which in turn arises out of prior conditions.

Buddhism is not to be equated with these elemental teachings of Gautama. Over 2,500 years many schools with their own distinctive teaching have evolved although three principal schools are commonly recognized: Theravāda, Māhayāna, and Tantrism. The Buddhist sutra itself mentions sixty-two sects.

Although Buddhism advances no dogmas or specific injunctions, there are traditional precepts to which the adherent commits himself if he wishes to achieve the way of life prescribed by Buddha, the middle way between asceticism and hedonism. Faith in the way is indispensable, but it is only a preliminary requirement for practicing the way. Faith can not to be contradictory to reason. In fact, it must be examined by reason lest it become superstition.

---

dhism," *Britannica*, 403–14. The *Britannica* devotes a total of sixty-six pages to Buddhism, its history, philosophy, and mysticism.

The middle path is known as the Noble Eight Fold Path, consisting of right view, right thought, right speech, right action, right mode of living, right endeavor, right mindfulness, and right concentration. In addition, there are Four Noble Truths. The first noble truth is the truth of misery, that man's existence is full of conflict, dissatisfaction, sorrow, and suffering. The second noble truth is that misery originates within us from selfish desire, craving for pleasure, or thirst. Attachment to these leads to rebirth. The third noble truth is that there is emancipation, liberation, and freedom from all of this which is the state of *Nirvāna*. *Nirvāna* is a transcendent state of freedom achieved by the extinction of desire and of individual consciousness. Whereas delusions of egocentricity and their resultant desires bind man to a continuous round of rebirths and suffering, release from these bonds constitutes enlightenment or the experience of *Nirvāna*. *Nirvāna* is conceived somewhat differently within the various schools of Budddhism. The fourth noble truth is that there exists a way to this liberation, namely, the Noble Eight Fold Path.

Siddhartha Gautama, having formulated what we know as his basic teachings, passed leisurely through cities and towns and villages of India where he immediately gained disciples for his movement and which he continued to do until an advanced age. Trained, learned, well-disciplined followers were soon to come. A monastic movement arose almost at once. Buddhism calls itself the Middle Path, explicitly avoiding the extremes of asceticism as well as the indulgences of ordinary life. Meditation is a practice of inward concentration, regulated to facilitate insight based on doctrinal understanding.

One who has faith in the teachings of Buddha and lives in accord with those teachings passes through three identifiable stages. First, he who has entered the stream, that is, has begun the process leading to rebirth can take two paths: that of devotion and that of intellectual discipline. His chances of rebirth are reduced greatly. Second comes the stage of one who returns only once. The third stage is that of one who does not return again for he has freed himself from the lower bonds (belief in a permanent self, doubt, sensual passion, and malice). He can obtain liberation in the time that runs from rebirth in a paradise, or even while in this existence.[9]

Accepting and practicing the teachings of Buddha thus enables one to overcome the cycle of rebirths. Several qualities follow enlightenment: clear memory, a desire for the exact investigation of natural things, energy, sympathy, tranquillity, impartiality, and a disposition for concentration. In following the teachings of Buddha, the adherent gains freedom from death because he has accomplished all that he proposed and had to do in order to achieve his freedom. He is free from all bonds, including the desire for existence in the formed or formless worlds, excitability, ambition, and ignorance. He has achieved *Nirvāna*.

Buddhism is not a philosophy or religion in the Western sense but is rather a path. A buddha is simply one who has walked this path and reports to others what he has found. Yet Buddhism is both a system of thought and a set of ethical norms offering practical guidance to everyday life. We find within contemporary Buddhism a logic, an implicit metaphysics, a psychology, and an eschatology.

In the East, Buddhism, Jainism, and Ajivakas all emerged at the same time and from the same cultural network. Buddhism depends on the acceptance of the concepts of *karma* and "reincarnation." Having rejected the harshness of inherited forms of asceticism, Buddha's emphasis on moderate meditation practice greatly widened his recruitment base by making the life of a monk more

9. Giuseppe Tucci, "Buddhism," 377.

appealing. Monastic life in turn accommodated itself to the lay world. Although Buddhist monks were themselves withdrawn from the world into a monastic community, they at the same time made a place for continuing relationships with their lay supporters. Monasteries became agents for economic growth in the countryside. In this manner Buddhism laid down a basic cultural framework for lay society, which eventually became Hinduism.

Buddha accepted the idea of *karma,* a chain of causality which leads to attachment to the forms of the material world and hence to rebirth. *Karma* was thought of as inescapable fate: each person's life goes through its chain of consequences and rebirths until it reaches its end. Indians had suffered for centuries under a pessimistic belief that they were bound to a wheel of rebirths in a suffering world and were bound too by an oppressive caste system. Buddha showed the way to liberation.

Buddha embraced an inherited idea of causation, namely, the momentariness of all phenomena. All things are caused by dependent origination, therefore nothing has an essence of its own, standing outside the stream of causation. Everything is void. There is neither future nor past, nor any motion. Everything is substanceless.

Mahayana Buddhism turned away from the prolonged meditative practices of the monks. It elevated the ceremonial taking of vows, which might also be taken by lay persons. The physical text of Buddhist teachings itself became the focus of ritual worship: copying and reciting scriptures became major acts of religious merit.

It is easy to understand why many consider Buddhism to be a religion. It has many of the cultural, social, and artistic trappings associated with Western religion. In common with Western religion from classical Greece and Rome, there is the moral admonition to moderation and self-restraint. In common with Christianity, one finds a premium placed on contemplation and withdrawal as a means to self-perfection that fostered monasteries. Shrines and art work perpetuate the memory of Buddha, as do temples and monuments venerate major figures in the history of Christianity. There are sacred texts to be preserved. But there the comparison fails. But the key element, an acknowledgment of God's existence and its implications in worship, is nowhere to be found. From the moral point of view, conquering self has an entirely different meaning from what it has in Stoic or Christian outlooks. Without the concept of immateriality or a human soul, there is no possibility of ultimate union with a personal God. Monastic life differs too insofar as Western monasticism is devoted to worship, which is the self turned outward, whereas Eastern monasticism is devoted to contemplation, which is the self turned inward. Whereas Hebraic and Christian scriptures are regarded as divine revelation, there is no such attribution to the ancient texts revered in Buddhism. To place Buddhism and Western religion within a single category is to ignore a difference between affirmation and denial. The sociological term "cultural vehicle" may cover both, but it must be acknowledged that "religion" is a decidedly Western term, a Latin term that indicates the payment of debt to God.

This brief treatment of Buddhism is not meant to reveal its many facets but is designed to show that from certain premises regarding nature and human nature, certain practices logically follow. Seeking *Nirvāna* is based on the doctrine of transitory existence. Without the acceptance of *karma* and "reincarnation," the Noble Eight Fold Path does not follow nor does the monastic movement associated with Buddhism. Worship is not enjoined because the existence of God is not acknowledged. Even in its admonition to moderation, Buddhism is essentially materialistic.

THE UNITY OF RELIGIOUS
EXPERIENCE

The focus of this study is Western religion. Its salient features, however, are analogously present in Eastern religion and other cultural expressions. Considerations of Eastern religion and primitive religion are instructive, indeed indispensable, in understanding the logic of religion. Yet the far greater mass of material available for the study of Western culture leads naturally to its exemplar status as we consider the distinctive features of religion. Our knowledge of the West is more intimate and internal as is evident from the authors who are considered in this discussion. The other great world cultures have achieved their own synthesis between religion and life, but Western civilization, as Christopher Dawson has shown in his classic study of medieval civilization, has been the great ferment of change in the world. The achievements of modern science and technology arose in the West for reasons inherent in the Christian culture that supplanted that of Greece and Rome.[1]

Commentators, philosophers, and historians through the ages have recognized that religion begins with the acceptance of a set of beliefs, intellectual in character, the implications of which imme-

1. Christopher Dawson, *Religion and the Rise of Western Culture* (New York: Doubleday, 1991).

diately find their way into the practical order. In every generation religion is inherited, but its distant origins can usually be traced to a founder or founding revelation. The great monotheisms of the West present themselves as the conduits of divine revelation. Recorded or synthesized, that revelation creates a sacred literature that preserves a basic teaching for subsequent generations. As presented in Judaic, Christian, and Muslim texts, God is thought to have disclosed himself in human history and to have proposed a set of laws for universal human observance. Those texts, while adding revealed knowledge, subtract nothing from the wealth of classical learning used to unlock and to develop their meanings. In the case of Christianity it is to be remembered that the New Testament was written in Greek, not in the Hebrew of Moses and the prophets, nor in the Aramaic of Jesus and His disciples, nor yet in the Latin of Imperial Rome, but in the Greek of Socrates and Plato.

Personal assent to revelation or to the teaching of a master entails both an intellectual and an affective response. This is particularly true of Christianity where revelation is found in the God-Man Christ whose person as well as teaching is disclosed in the Gospels and Acts of the Apostles. The kings and prophets of ancient Israel are personages that at once lend themselves to art and literature and create an affective bond between the hearer and the message. Many today, young and old, carry the names of Abraham, Isaac, Jacob, David, Sarah, Rachel, Susanna, Ann, and Daniel.

Following a common acknowledgment of revealed truth or of the truth of a master's teachings, a community of believers naturally emerges. Common acknowledgment in the case of the biblical religions leads to both individual and communal acts. Acknowledgment of the divine origin of human life and the brotherhood of mankind generates in the practical order beneficent activity which extends even beyond the community of believers. These Aquinas called "the secondary acts of religion," acts such as charity, the care of the sick, the elderly, widows, and orphans. Worship in its various manifestations such as prayer and sacrifice Aquinas recognized as primary.

Common acknowledgment inevitably leads to visible institutions, temples, synagogues, and churches that not only serve as centers of worship and homage but as conservers of doctrine. Historically, Christianity has inspired some of the greatest artistic achievement the world has known in architecture, painting, and music, appreciated by believers and nonbelievers. Much of the classical architecture and statuary admired today has its origin in reverence for the gods and the eternal verities perpetuated in classical literature. The temples of ancient Greece and Rome, the cathedrals of medieval Christendom, and the mosques of Islam draw tourists and pilgrims from around the globe. Museums throughout the West prominently display sculpture from the classical period and paintings inspired by the biblical narratives as well as contemporary artifacts which draw upon those traditions. Nonbelievers can be as appreciative of religious art as believers. Auguste Comte appreciated the ritual traditions of Christianity. George Santayana loved to meditate while seated in the Basilica of San Giovanni in Laterano, the pope's own Church, amidst the baroque Titans lining its columns. Leonard Bernstein, a Jewish composer, has written a Catholic Mass. Westerners similarly appreciate art that draws upon the religious and cultural traditions of the East.

No religion or other moral or intellectual tradition is without dissenters within its ranks. Christianity was rent by schism in its early centuries. The Protestant revolt against Rome has spawned hundreds of sects that still call themselves Christian. Modern Judaism is divided into orthodox, conservative, and reformed congregations. Similar divisions are found within Islam. Without a teaching authority or authoritative body, mutations render the body ineffective as a tutor and undermine liturgical cohesiveness. Each religious body strives to protect its unity in its own way, sometimes politically or by an emphasis on ethnic identity.

All major religious bodies have had to contend with those who would reduce their transcendent source and spiritual message to a purely naturalistic or secular one. The twelfth-century Islamic philosopher Averroes (1126–98) distinguished between levels of understanding, relegating to theology the role of making accessible to the masses the natural truths discovered by philosophy. Distinguishing among religion, theology, and philosophy, Averroes held that these are but three modes of discourse corresponding to the three classes of men. *Religion* is truth made accessible to the common man who must be induced to live virtuously by eloquent preaching, that is, by appeals made to the imagination rather than to the intellect. *Theology* is the attempted rational justification of common belief, but it is only *philosophy* that provides the nucleus of truth contained in the fancies of the men of faith. The three approaches to the same truth ultimately agree with one another. The beliefs of the common people and the teachings of the theologians are simply philosophical truths adapted to inferior minds.

Yet Averroes did not consider religion to be merely a rough approximation of philosophic truth. For him, it was much more. It had a definite social function that could not be fulfilled by anything else, not even by philosophy. The Koran he believed to be a miraculous book and one "divinely inspired" because he found it more effective than philosophy in raising people to the level of morality. Thus, Moses, Jesus, and Mohammed can be considered true prophets and messengers of God to mankind; but their religions were only popular approaches to the truth found in its purity in philosophy.

This position was to be partially reiterated in Hegel's all-embracing system in which Christian faith was treated as a moment in the unfolding of Absolute Spirit. For Hegel, religious language expresses in a symbolic manner the universality of truth that philosophy alone brings to rational explicitness. The leading French deists of the Enlightenment period did not simply reject revelation. Rather they sought to show that its genuine content was identical with natural religion as opposed to revealed religion, specifically Christianity.

The socially cohesive force of religion is recognized by believers and nonbelievers, by historians and political theorists of every persuasion. Secular regimes recognize religion as a spiritual counter to their purely materialistic aims. Stalin's suppression of religion is well documented. China under its present regime is actively hostile to Christianity. When Germany was united after the fall of the Berlin Wall, West Germans found more than one generation of their countrymen from the East to be religiously illiterate, with social consequences distancing them from their fellow countrymen. In Germany at the close of the century unification remains more than an economic problem.

The hunger for the truth about the human condition continues unabated under suppressive regimes and eventually contributes to their demise. The importance of religion is then almost spontaneously recognized. In the West socialist regimes unchecked by the time-transcending truth conveyed by Christianity tend to become totalitarian. Without a moral compass, secular ritual replaces Christian tradition, pointing up another important element in human nature: the need for ritual, for celebration, for feast days. A religious context bestows a meaning which seems unavailable to the secular conscience. Earth Day is an impoverished substitute for the blessing of the fleet or of the crops. Celebrating the winter solstice does not manifest the warmth of Christmastide. A forced return to pagan motifs as a means of replacing Christian symbols rarely captures either the heart or the imagination.

Western civilization is so bound up with Christianity that it is difficult to separate the two. Its artistic inspiration is apparent to all. More subtly, in providing a concept of nature, human nature, and the relation between the two, Christianity laid the conceptual foundation for modern science by providing an understanding of *theoria* and *praxis* that Greek intelligence failed to do. In common with the Greek, Christianity has taught that nature is intelligible and that its secrets are open to painstaking investigation. But historians of science and technology point to this difference: Christianity insisted that the fruits of inquiry are to be employed in the interest of alleviating the burden of the worker, whereas the Greeks too-speculative approach to nature are thought by many historians of science and technology to have prevented the use of science to create new technology. The Benedictines have been called the first intellectuals in the history of the West to get dirt under their fingernails. It is in the monasteries founded by St. Benedict that we have a witness to the emergence of an intellectual outlook different from both classical and Eastern Christian approaches.[2] It is well known that the Benedictine monasteries played a crucial role in the development of Western culture. From the decline of Roman civilization to the rise of the European universities in the twelfth century, a period of approximately seven hundred years, the monasteries were to play an indispensable role not only as bearers of classical learning but as cultivators of science and technology in their own right. The educational institutions of the Roman Empire were swept away by the barbarian invasions as they declined and died with the declining city culture of the Latin world. It was only in the monasteries that the Latin classics were preserved. The

2. Cf. Jude P. Dougherty, "Intellectuals with Dirt under Their Fingernails," *Communio*, Fall 1982, 225–37.

monastic schools and libraries and *scriptoria* became the chief organs of the higher intellectual culture in Western Europe. By the sixteenth century, more than seven hundred monasteries dotted the European landscape. As early as the middle of the twelfth century, the cathedral schools began to vie with the monasteries as centers of learning and cultural influence. As competition among the monastic schools increased, the network of teachers divided itself into specialized organizations in their own right, and formed universities specializing in philosophy and theology. While much of the learning fostered in the monastic and cathedral schools was theological and scriptural, still there was no lack of the kind of learning we would today call humanistic. Nor was there the absence of technological innovation.

If there is a logic to religion, there is also a logic to anti-religion. The revolutionary socialism of the nineteenth century in contrast to Christianity has led to moral and social chaos wherever it has gained political ascendancy. Committed to a narrow range of beliefs (atheism, materialism, and some form of social engineering), it has led to intellectual and artistic sterility and frequently to both cultural and economic impoverishment under the regimes which have adopted its ideology, viz., the former Soviet Union, Castro's Cuba, and North Korea. Examples of cultural and economic impoverishment are abundant. Were that that were all. The twentieth century has been the bloodiest in human history. Those most responsible for the killing have been atheists who explicitly rejected any religiously based idea that human life is sacred or more than a tool in the name of their ideologically driven programs. Socialist regimes overlook spiritual issues at their peril. History shows clearly that it makes a difference whether one regards human rights as divinely bestowed and therefore unconditional or as a *modus vivendi* born of a social contract. Under a socialist regime, rights are precarious.

While the philosopher cannot point to the truth of any revealed religion, he can recognize consistency in doctrine and coherence with what is otherwise known to be true. Some philosophies open one to the transcendent; others reject it as an intellectual option. Marx, Freud, and Dewey exemplify in their hostility to religion the logical conclusion of their materialism. The type of philosophy one espouses, implicitly or explicitly, either opens one to faith or closes faith as an intellectual option. Furthermore, the type of philosophy one espouses determines the kind of Christianity one embraces. Classical Greek and Roman intelligence gave rise to, and forever will lead to, the institution shaped by the Fathers and Doctors of the early and medieval Church. If one starts with modern philosophical nominalism or epistemology, one will not end up in the belief system that shaped Aquinas and to which the Parisian master contributed. The differences between Plato and Aristotle, for example, or between realism and nominalism, are carried through history as Christians attempt to understand their faith. Ancient skepticisms and Pyrrhonism have their modern counterparts that make belief as impossible today as those outlooks made it impossible in antiquity. Clearly the presence or absence of religion in a people makes a moral and inevitably a cultural difference. The cultural legacy of Greece and Rome is reflected not only in the art and architecture that bear witness to it, but also in the development of early Christianity. Eastern religions, drawing upon an entirely different intellectual outlook, were shaped in a different manner. But, as we have seen, commonalities persist.

It would be foolish to regard all religious claims as equally grounded. The value of any religious claim can be scrutinized for its rationality. Error and superstition are to be found within any comprehensive body of doctrine and practice. But some religious bodies are better at guarding their integrity than others. Some only imperfectly grasp what is thought to have been revealed or what is thought to be essential to its care.

Philosophy, with its techniques of description, definition, and ability to distinguish and to draw inferences can be of help to any religious mind or religious community as it attempts to understand and develop its key doctrines. Theology is impossible without philosophy. Philosophy, as we have attempted to show, can both illuminate the inner structure of religion and, drawing upon the experience of centuries, can say something about the role of religion in society.

Any philosophy which offers itself as an alternative or substitute for religion is presumptuous and is apt to deprive the human intellect of an important avenue of knowledge, not to mention dampen the human spirit and darken artistic and cultural vistas. We end with the observation that although its object be God, religion is a human invention subject to all the vagaries which characterize human endeavor. The Christian would admit as much but then claim that the God-Man Christ came to show a way unavailable to human reason alone. That claim cannot be falsified and will forever be a stumbling block or a source of inspiration as it has for two thousand years.

Bibliography

Ahern, Emily Martin. *Chinese Ritual and Politics.* Cambridge: Cambridge University Press, 1981.

Anderson-Gold, Sharon. "Unnecessary Evil: History and Moral Progress," in *The Philosophy of Immanuel Kant.* Albany: State University of New York Press, 2001.

Babbitt, Irving. *Rousseau and Romanticism,* Intro. by Claes G. Ryn. New Brunswick, NJ: Transaction Publications, 1991.

Beck, Lewis White. *Essays on Kant and Hume.* New Haven: Yale University Press, 1978.

Bethune-Baker, James F. *Introduction to the Early History of Christian Doctrine.* London: Methuen, 1903.

Blumenberg, Hans. *The Legitimacy of the Modern Age.* Cambridge: MIT Press, 1983.

Bochenski, Joseph M. *The Logic of Religion.* New York: New York University Press, 1967.

Boyarin, Jonathan. *Thinking in Jewish.* Chicago: University of Chicago Press, 1996.

Breuer, Mordechai. *Modernity within Tradition: A Social History of Orthodox Jewry in Imperial Germany.* New York: Columbia University Press, 1992.

Choper, Jesse H. *Principles for Judicial Interpretation of the Religion Clauses.* Chicago: University of Chicago Press, 1995.

Cicero, Marcus Tullius. *On the Commonwealth and On the Laws.* Ed. by James G. Zetzel. Cambridge: Cambridge University Press, 1999.

Collins, James. *Three Paths in Philosophy.* Chicago: Henry Regnery, 1962.

_____. *The Emergence of Philosophy of Religion.* New Haven, CT: Yale University Press, 1967.

Copelston, Frederick. *A History of Philosophy, Vol. VI: Wolff to Kant.* Westminster, MD: The Newman Press, 1960.

Dawson, Christopher. *Progress and Religion.* Garden City, NY: Doubleday (Image Book), 1960.

_____. *The Gods of the Revolution.* New York: New York University Press, 1972.

de Vries, Jan. *The Study of Religion.* New York: Harcourt, Brace and World, Inc., 1967.

Dupré, Louis. *The Other Dimension.* New York: Doubleday, 1972.

Durkheim, Emile. *The Elementary Forms of Religious Life.* London: George Allen and Unwin, Ltd., 1915.

Evans, C. Stephen. *Kierkegaard's Fragments and Postscripts: The Religious Philosophy of Johannes Climacus.* Atlantic Highlands, NJ: Humanities Press, 1983.

Fackenheim, Emil L. *Jewish Philosophers and Jewish Philosophy.* Bloomington, IN: Indiana University Press, 1996.

Feuérbach, Ludwig. *Das Wesen des Christentum* [*The Essence of Christianity*]. Trans. by George Eliot. New York: Harper & Row, 1957.

Fichte, Johann Gottlieb. *Attempt at a Critique of All Religion (Versucheiner Knitikaller Offenbarung).* Trans. by Garett Green. Cambridge: Cambridge University Press, 1978.

Frank, Daniel H., ed. *A People Apart: Closeness and Ritual in Jewish Philosophical Thought.* Albany: State University of New York Press, 1993.

———. *Autonomy and Judaism.* Albany: State University of New York Press, 1992.

Freud, Sigmund. *Die Zunkunft einer Illusion* (1927) [*The Future of an Illusion*]. Ed. by A. H. Brill. New York: Modern Library, 1938.

Gross, T. H. *Natural History of Religion.* London: Longmans, Green, 1912.

Guyer, Paul. *Kant on Freedom, Law, and Happiness.* New York: Cambridge University Press, 2000.

Hannay, A. and Marino, G. D., eds. *The Cambridge Companion to Kierkegaard.* Cambridge: The University Press, 1995.

Harrison, June. *Prolegomena to the Study of Greek Religion.* Cleveland: World Publishing Co., 1966.

Hegel, Georg W. F. *Lectures on the Philosophy of Religion,* 2 vols. Ed. by Peter C. Hodgson, trans. by R. F. Brown, P. C. Hodgson, and J. M. Stewart. Berkeley: University of California Press, 1984 and 1987.

———. *Three Essays, 1973–1795,* ed. and trans. by Peter Fuss and John Dobbins (Notre Dame: University of Notre Dame Press, 1984). These are translations of the Tübingen and Berne otherwise untitled lectures.

Hexter, J. H. *The Judaeo-Christian Tradition,* 2nd ed. New Haven, CT: Yale University Press, 1995.

Hume, David. *Dialogues Concerning Natural Religion.* Ed. by Norman Kemp Smith. Indianapolis: Bobbs-Merrill, 1947.

Hyman, Arthur, ed., *Maimonidean Studies.* New York: Yeshiva University Press, 1990.

James, William. *Varieties of Religious Experience.* New York: Longmans, Green, 14th impression, 1907.

Kant, Immanuel. *The Metaphysics of Morals* (1797). Intro., trans., and notes by Mary Gregor. Cambridge: Cambridge University Press, 1991.

———. *Religion and Rational Theology.* Trans. and ed. by Allen W. Wood and George di Giovanni. Cambridge: Cambridge University Press, 1996.

———. *Critique of Power of Judgment.* Ed. by Paul Guyer; trans. by P. Guyer and E. Matthews. Cambridge: Cambridge University Press, 2000.

Katz, Jacob. "The Role of Religion in Modern Jewish History," in *Proceedings of Regional Conferences of the Association for Jewish Studies.* Toronto: March–April, 1974.

Kierkegaard, Søren. *Concluding Unscientific Postscript.* Princeton: Princeton University Press, 1941.

_____. *Journals.* Ed. by Alexander Dru, New York: Harper & Row, 1964.

_____. *Repetition.* Trans. by Walter Lowrie. New York: Harper & Row, 1964.

Levine, Alan, ed. *Early Modern Skepticism and the Origins of Toleration.* Lanham, MD: Lexington Books, 1999.

Long, Eugene Thomas, ed. *God, Secularization, and History.* Columbia, SC: University of South Carolina Press, 1974.

Löwith, Karl. *From Hegel to Nietzsche: The Revolution in 19th Century Thought.* New York: Columbia University Press, 1991.

Maimonides. *The Guide of the Perplexed.* Ed. by Julius Guttman, trans. by Chaim Rabin. Indianapolis: Hackett Publishing Co., 1995.

Marx, Karl, and Engels, F. *The Communist Manifesto.* Trans. by Paul M. Sweezy. New York: Monthly Review Press, 1864.

Mill, John Stuart. *Theism.* Ed. by Richard Raylor. Indianapolis: Bobbs-Merrill, 1957.

_____. *Nature and Utility of Religion,* 3rd ed. London: Longmans, 1885.

_____. *Utilitarianism.* Ed. by Oskar Piest. Indianapolis: Bobbs-Merrill, 1957.

Nylan, Michael. *The Five "Confucian" Classics.* New Haven, CT: Yale University Press, 2001.

Palmer, Michael. *Freud and Jung on Religion.* New York: Routledge, 1997.

Pelican, Jaroslav. *Christianity and Classical Culture.* New Haven, CT: Yale University Press, 1999.

Purcell Jr., Edward A. *Brandeis and the Progressive Constitution: Erie, the Judicial Power and the Politics of the Federal Courts in Twentieth Century America.* New Haven, CT: Yale University Press, 1999.

Randall Jr., John Herman. *The Meaning of Religion for Man.* New York: Harper & Row, 1968.

Rose, Gillian. *Judaism and Modernity.* Oxford: Blackwell, 1993.

Rousseau, Jean-Jacques. *The Social Contract (1762).* Hammondsworth, England: Penguin Books, 1975.

_____. *The Basic Political Writings.* Indianapolis: Hackett, 1987.

_____. *Emile (1762).* Trans. by B. Foxley. London: Everyman's Library.

Ryn, Claes G. "Virtue Real and Imagined," in *The Unbought Grace of Life: Essays in Honor of Russell Kirk.* Ed. by James E. Person. LaSalle, IL: Sherwood Sugden, 1994, 115–36.

_____. "Imaginative Origins of Modernity: Life as Daydream and Nightmare," in *Humanitas,* Vol. X, No. 2, 1997, 41–60.

Santayana, George. "The Winds of Doctrine," in *The Works of George Santayana.* New York: Charles Scribner's Sons, 1937.

Schimmel, Annemarie. *Islam: An Introduction.* Albany, NY: State University of New York Press, 1992.

Smart, Ninian, ed. *Nineteenth Century Religious Thought,* 3 vols. Cambridge: Cambridge University Press, 1985.

Smith, Barry, ed. "Christian Philosophy," *The Monist.* Vol. 75, no. 3. Special issue ed. by Joseph Owens.

Strauss, Leo. *Spinoza's Critique of Religion.* Chicago: University of Chicago Press, 1997.

Strodach, George K., trans. *The Philosophy of Epicurus.* Evanston, IL: Northwestern University Press, 1963.

Walsh, David. *The Third Millennium: Reflections on Faith and Reason.* Washington, DC: Georgetown University Press, 1999.

Wippel, John F. *The Metaphysical Thought of Thomas Aquinas.* Washington, DC: The Catholic University of America Press, 2000.

Index

The Logic of Religion was designed and composed in Minion with Hiroshige display type by Kachergis Book Design of Pittsboro, North Carolina. It was printed on sixty-pound Glatfelter Natural and bound by Cushing-Malloy, Inc., Ann Arbor, Michigan.